THE
Old-
Fashioned
FRUIT
GARDEN

THE *Old-Fashioned* FRUIT GARDEN

THE BEST WAY TO GROW, PRESERVE, AND BAKE WITH SMALL FRUIT

Jo Ann Gardner

Foreword by Jigs Gardner

Skyhorse Publishing

Originally published in Canada by Nimbus Publishing

www.skyhorsepublishing.com

10 9 8 7 6 5 4 3 2 1

Library of Congress Cataloging-in-Publication Data available on file.

ISBN: 978-1-61608-621-3

Printed in China

This fruit of my labor is dedicated to Jigs,
beloved partner in all things.

To those who joy in their work,
this old earth laughs with them.

—Samuel Fraser, 1924

Contents

Author's Notes on a New Edition

Over forty years ago, in 1971, we moved ourselves, our four children, and a Noah's Ark of animals to a remote farm at the northeastern tip of Nova Scotia, to Cape Breton Island. We wanted to own a piece of earth where we could grow our food and keep some poultry and livestock, as we had been doing at rented farms. We were tired of planting strawberries and not being around to harvest them because the landlord sold the place where we were living, but with the money we saved we hadn't been able to afford anything suitable in the northeastern U.S. where Jigs and I had always lived.

We had no idea, really, of what we would be up against in Cape Breton: long, gray, maritime winters of freezing and thawing; heavy clay soil, slow to warm and leached of nutrients; and wind . . . oh, the wind, enough to blow our little greenhouse roof off, not once, but three times. I know, because I helped, in a roaring wind, to nail it back down.

I haven't mentioned income, because for the first five years, we hadn't any. We lived on our savings, and we lived a very lean life. After the first year, the bad roads shook up our old truck so much we abandoned it and used our team of horses wherever we needed to go, not very far. I called our backlands farm the No Capitol of the World: no vehicle, no running water (Jigs, ever creative, tells me it did run . . . out of the hand pump), and no phone. We did have electricity, but not a very sound system and we did not tax it much. We heated and cooked solely with wood and we had no freezer.

But there is no reason to be sorry for those years. We learned so much. Not only about Canada, and Cape Breton and its folk culture, of which we were sublimely ignorant, but about ourselves and how far we could stretch our abilities. In 1978 when the youngest of our children left the farm, I found myself to be the only other hand on staff. With no prior experience (I graduated from Bennington, majoring in drama and literature), with pitchfork in hand, standing on the hay wagon that Jigs drove around the field, I learned to build tons of hay each summer and helped to unload them in the barn. I pulled at the other end of a cross-cut saw to cut down huge trees for firewood . . . when Jigs pointed in the direction I was to run after the tree cracked, you can be sure I ran fast. I learned to spread manure by moonlight with the team of horses after a day in the woods, a day that also included barn chores (milking, cleaning out pens, feeding, and watering) and cooking three big meals a day.

Those were also the years of enormous fruit harvests. Early on, we had built two log cabins for guests to bring in some income, and before breakfast, they might pick buckets of gooseberries or baskets and baskets of raspberries that had to be turned to account as fast as I could manage. With no freezer, I adapted older recipes to suit my circumstances; readers may appreciate how I dispensed with topping and tailing gooseberries. And somehow I managed not only to preserve the fruit harvest but produce superior products. What I learned became the source of inspiration for *The Old-Fashioned Fruit Garden*, the first edition of this book, published in 1989.

A lot has happened in the intervening years. In 2001, for one thing, we moved back to the States, to the foothills of the Adirondacks, in New York's Champlain Valley. We live now in a converted one-room schoolhouse with 10, instead of 100 acres of land, and we keep flocks of poultry. We still maintain large gardens that mostly feed us, we raise as much fruit as we can, and we still enjoy foraging in the wild. The principles that unconsciously drove us—simplicity, economy, and self-reliance—are still in practice, imprinted on our souls. Looking back, I see that we were green when green was just a color, but we didn't live 'green' on principle. Our lives grew out of our preferences. We followed a path of our own desire. Whatever we did and however we have lived, for better or for worse, there is no pretension about it. It just *is*.

A lot has happened, too, in the field of fruit development. There are many new varieties (more correctly, cultivars) among traditional June-bearing, everbearing, and day-neutral strawberries, for instance, so that the home gardener has the possibility of harvesting more than one crop a season; the same is true of raspberries, among the fall-bearing type. And blackberries are coming along with similar characteristics.

Among fruit trees, there are more semi-dwarf types that take up far less room than standards, and there are even some that can be grown in tubs. Blueberries, a beautiful bush in flower, whose leaves turn bright scarlet in the fall, have been the subject of breeding and selection to find ever more beautiful and productive varieties.

In general, the breeding trend is toward fruits that are not only productive, disease and insect resistant, and adaptable to different conditions, but ones that have ornamental value. Landscaping with edibles is definitely a trend among home gardeners.

Today, a significant number of gardeners are interested in growing less common fruits. As Tim Malinich, Extension Educator of the Lorain County Extension Office in Ohio told me, "Ten years ago, if I did a talk and mentioned elderberries or currants a few people would have had experience or interest. Today, a significant number of gardeners either have experience with or are willing to work with less common fruits such as currants, elderberries, and gooseberries. In fact, it is becoming almost trendy to grow them." Their health benefits, too (along with blueberries), have been in the news, altogether giving these fruits a higher profile.

This new edition of *The Old-Fashioned Fruit Garden* takes into account all these trends—in fruit breeding and interest in the less common fruits—and offers one of the most comprehensive collections of recipes and directions for preserving and using currants (including a hefty section on black currants), gooseberries, and elderberries, for these were the very fruits that were the backbone of our Cape Breton gardens. What was old-fashioned is now new. I have added quince to the mix, an old-fashioned tree that seems to me elegant enough to grow just for looks, but I do include recipes.

Along with the many recipes for making jellies and jams with no commercial pectin added (these are now called "artisan" products), the hallmark of this book, I have added new ones like Ginger-Peach Jam; more accompanying dairy products like Yogurt and Yogurt Cheese Spread that you can make even without a cow tethered in your front yard; and directions for making fruit sherberts, sorbets, and frozen fruit yogurts (the freezer is modestly featured in this edition). On a hot summer's day, you may want to make my Black Currant Sorbet and serve it, as I suggest, embellished with a fresh-picked, edible Zebrina flower (*Malva sylvestris* Zebrina), a lovely rose-pink with purple stripes.

To meet the current high standards for home fruit preserving, I have updated directions to include the latest information from the current *Ball's Blue Book Guide to Preserving* (2011).

The new Appendix takes into account the Internet (I have also included phone numbers wherever possible). There you will find sources for contacting your nearest Cooperative Extension office; finding the nearest U-Pick operation if you don't have your own garden (you could also consider bartering from someone who does); where to find uncommon fruit plants and heirloom seeds for growing citron ("the preserving melon"); Pyola, an organic insecticide that works; where to find canning equipment and the latest new pectins that don't take a lot of sugar or any (you can adapt my recipes); cheese-making supplies to make all the dairy products I discuss in the book: and the hand tools to make truly artisan fruit products. I have not forgotten Canadian readers and have included Canadian sources, too.

I am thrilled to offer a new generation of fruit growers and preservers, the novice and the experienced, this new edition of *The Old-Fashioned Fruit Garden.* I trust that those who loved the old edition will find a place for the new one, too, on the shelves of their gardening/cookbook library.

Westport, New York, 2012

Acknowledgments

I wish to thank the Horticultural Research Institute of Ontario at Vineland Station, the Agriculture Canada Research Station at Kentville, Nova Scotia, and the Agriculture Canada Research Station at Buctouche, New Brunswick, for providing me with information on the status of black currants in North America.

I am also indebted to the following institutes in the United States: the Connecticut Agricultural Experiment Station, the Missouri Cooperative Extension Service, the New York State Agricultural Experiment Station, the New York State Department of Environmental Conservation, the Rutgers Extension Service, the Maine Department of Conservation, the University of Alaska Agricultural Experiment Station, the University of Minnesota Agricultural Extension Service, the University of Rhode Island Cooperative Extension, the University of Wisconsin Extension Program, the United States Department of Agriculture, and the departments of agriculture of Michigan, New Hampshire, New Jersey, Oregon, and Vermont.

I would also like to thank Carol Makielski, formerly of the Makielski Berry Farm & Nursery in Michigan, and Michael McConkey of Edible Landscaping in Virginia for encouraging me in my promotion of black currants. I am indebted to the North American Fruit Explorers and the Brooklyn Botanical Garden Information Service for their help in this research.

I am grateful to those unnamed generations of cooks from whose creative genius I have freely borrowed, as well as to a few friends and guests whose recipes have enriched my repertoire.

I owe thanks to *Rural Delivery, Farmstead, Country Journal,* and *Harrowsmith,* which have previously published some of the material in this book in a different form.

I am thankful to Dorothy Blythe of Nimbus Publishing for her interest in a gardener's cookbook and to Nancy Robb for her editorial comments and suggestions. Any inconsistencies or idiosyncracies are my own.

Jo Ann Gardner
Orangedale, N.S., 1989

To the above, I add thanks to Tim Malinich, Extension Educator, Horticulture, of the Lorain County Extension Office, for sharing his views on plant breeding trends, trials of new blackberry cultivars, the status of black currants in his state, and more; and to Judy French of the Cornell Cooperative Extension office in Westport, New York, for her assistance. Special thanks to Lois Rose, Nell Gardner, Jeanne Leblanc, Bob Miller, Rob Demuro, and Russell Studebaker for their help in various ways, all important to me.

I am indebted to Jenn McCartney at Skyhorse for her patience in guiding me through the process of this new edition, and to Jigs, my partner-in-all-things, and an invaluable advisor on all literary points.

J. A. G., 2012

Foreword

I made my first jelly, wild grape, in Madison, Wisconsin, in the late summer of 1956. Exactly why, I cannot remember. That summer, we had our first garden, I was beginning to learn about wildflowers, and I was interested in making some of the things we usually bought, such as soap. Perhaps the recollection of my mother hanging a jelly bag from a broom handle suspended between two dining-room chairs helped inspire me.

I suppose that having seen some grapes on one of my wildflower rambles, I must have looked up a recipe. Luckily, this turned out to be a great jelly. If our first product had been ordinary or dull, our jam- and jelly-making careers might have developed more slowly.

I remember grape-picking expeditions with my wife, Jo Ann, and our one-year-old son, Seth: I'm in a tree dropping bunches of wild grapes to Jo Ann, who is tucking them into Seth's baby carriage. Then the three of us are wandering through an overgrown, abandoned quarry, picking grapes from vines on crumbling stone walls.

I have another wild-grape memory, of quite a different sort; I'm crouching under a big bush on a side street in Madison, picking grapes from a vine growing over the bush. A man stops beside the bush, peers under, and asks me what I'm doing. He turns out to be an acquaintance who runs a bookstore downtown. While I crouch in the green shade under the bush and he stands on the sidewalk in the bright sun, we have a small, friendly debate that, although I did not know it then, I would have over and over again, and not just about jams and jellies, either.

He thought that making my own jelly was foolish because (1) I could buy it in a store for less than the cost of making it; (2) the time spent picking and processing grapes could be used to earn more money than my jelly would be worth; and (3) crouching under a bush in broad daylight in a modern city was really, well, nutty looking.

That was the first time I engaged in that debate, and I'm afraid I did not give effective answers, although I do remember pointing out that I preferred to spend my time picking wild fruit than earning money. I also said that I could not buy superior jelly anywhere. Now, however, having been through this argument scores of times, I know other things to say: my time is as valuably spent picking wild fruit and making excellent nutritious preserves as it is doing anything else; I do not want to give up a significant portion of my life for a wage so that I can buy a jar of sweetened chemicals; when we make our own food, we *know* it is good; and, finally, I have learned not to worry about being nutty looking. There are thousands of people walking around loose today doing worse-looking things than crouching under a bush and picking wild grapes.

For some years, when I was a teacher and had summers off, I did the jam and jelly making, as well as all the other canning and preserving, for our growing family. In the early 1960s, we began to sell some jams and jellies. But when we started farming and founded a school, there was a radical reorganization of the division of labor in our family. Jo Ann took over my kitchen tasks, and all our preserves improved. She had more mouths to feed, larger gardens to process, as well as meat, produce, and dairy products to sell. In 1971, we moved to Cape Breton. Not only did we have a farm to run, we also began to rent log cabins to visitors. So Jo Ann had more meals to cook, and they had to be first rate.

When I come in from the stables or fields nowadays, I am, at most, Jo Ann's assistant, sometimes washing up after butter making or drawing off whey from cheese or packing away case after case of jam. It is just as well. As our many guests and customers will testify, Jo Ann is a good cook: intelligent, hard working, and sensible. I, on the other hand, usually give in to anarchic tendencies in the kitchen, disregarding directions in a fine frenzy of creative disaster. But I will not go into my mistakes. Follow Jo Ann's directions exactly, and you will make excellent jams, jellies, sasses, juices, and fresh-fruit preserves.

Jigs Gardner
Orangedale, N.S., 1989

Introduction

When was the last time you tasted some absolutely terrific homemade jam, the kind that made you want to try making it, too? I do not mean freezer jam or some concoction made with Jell-O or commercial pectin and loads of sugar. I mean the real thing: jam made with fresh berries that are mashed, heated with just enough sugar to bring out the fresh-fruit flavor, brought to a boil, and cooked for no more than 15 minutes (usually less), until the mixture has thickened.

Jam making, like other kinds of fruit preserving, has become almost a lost art superseded by the mass production and marketing of fruit products in the supermarket. At one time, 100, 75, even 50 years ago, the fruit garden, like the vegetable garden, supplied a great part of the family's food needs. Many backyards and almost all farms had fruiting shrubs, a rhubarb patch, and a variety of apple trees to provide fruit for baking, cooking, drying, or storing. Few women in these households did not know how to turn their garden fruits into an astonishing number of concoctions—jams, jellies, preserves, conserves, marmalades, sauces, juices, wines, vinegars, dried fruits—astonishing when compared with the paucity of products offered in today's markets. Have you ever tried to buy red currant sauce or gooseberry preserves—or fresh gooseberries, for that matter?

The "plucky housewife" of the turn of the century preserved from necessity because processed foods were not readily available.

Home preserving was a serious business and one in which the homemaker took great pride. There was a lot of skill involved in choosing varieties of fruits for different purposes. Take pears, for instance: the Winter Nellis was known for storing; the Pound, for eating; and the Bartlett, for flavor. How many women, or men, today know one variety from another or can even find each in the marketplace?

Jam making is probably the last vestige of home fruit preserving, but the skills that were once an absolute necessity for turning out successful products have been neglected in the almost universal desire to emulate mass-produced store-bought varieties. For the unskilled, foolproof methods such as using commercial pectin and the freezer guarantee a "successful" product every time.

What are the qualities of store-bought preserves? In jam, they include a heavy sweet taste, an overfirm set, an absence of real fruit flavor—in sum, a general lack of all distinction. Unfortunately, the word *homemade* is no longer synonymous with all the superior qualities. No doubt, among the home-processed fruit products of the past, there were a lot of duds: burned jams, runny jellies, moldy preserves. But when the household itself depended on and processed all the fruit for the family, quality—the kind associated with the best of homemade—counted.

There may be some merit in the Victorian notion that tending a garden, watching plants grow, has an ennobling influence. But there are other compelling reasons for creating your own fruit garden, that is, an old-fashioned garden that can supply you and your family with almost all your fruit needs.

First, there is the reason of economy: fruit and fruit products can be expensive for a growing family. If a small fruit garden can supply products as good, or better, as the supermarket at much less expense, it makes a lot of sense to consider making even small plots productive. Wild fruits should not be overlooked: abandoned orchards can yield truckloads of apples for cider, wild grapes can make an incomparable jelly, staghorn sumac can supply a tart lemonlike flavor for juice.

Second, the quality of fruit bought in a store cannot compare to the quality of fruit from a garden. Store-bought fruit is not so fresh; consider as well the handling and shipping and the heavy use of pesticides. Have you ever compared the taste of a California strawberry out of season with one just picked from your own patch? Have you ever tasted raspberry juice, jam, or ice cream made from real raspberries, not from a concentrate or "flavor" whipped up in a food chemist's lab? You cannot even find gooseberry or black currant products in most ordinary stores; even the fancy gourmet products are inferior to those you can make yourself from the harvest of old-fashioned fruiting shrubs. To avoid making products with a store-bought taste, however, you must follow the simple preserving methods described later in this book.

Third, there is the important consideration of energy use and conservation. Do you really think that small is beautiful, that less is more, that technology should be carefully, not wantonly, used, that resources should be husbanded, not squandered, that we must learn to live in harmony with the natural world?

The old-fashioned fruit garden can point the way by showing you how to achieve energy efficiency through the best use of simple technology. Only those fruits most suitable to one's environment are grown; they are harvested for particular uses and processed by the simplest means to achieve a superior product.

Is it absolutely necessary to "pop" food in the freezer or "toss" it into the blender when other techniques less demanding of energy, less destructive to the land, are accessible? Before World War II, people used noninstant powdered milk, knives for cutting and chopping, hand food mills for puréeing, and rotary beaters for beating.

I do not advocate going back in time, but we must begin to think about how we use technology. The care with which we do this will be reflected in a higher quality of life, a life more in tune with the natural world rather than antagonistic toward it. Growing and processing your own fruit, taking as little from the land as possible while creating the conditions for continual renewal and regrowth, is immensely satisfying and ecologically sound. "The land," wrote Liberty Hyde Bailey, the great American horticulturist, "is the cemetery of the ages and the resurrection of all life."

Technology constantly changes, and just as there have been many improvements made by plant breeders in creating vigorous, disease-resistant fruit varieties, so has modern industry produced superior equipment and techniques for home processing. But I leave the electric dehydrators and similar devices to the do-it-yourself sophisticates. The technology I have in mind really *is* simple and within reach of most people.

Canning and jelly jars with vacuum-sealing snap lids and screw bands are a great improvement over older kinds of jars and closures and ensure successful preserving if directions are carefully followed.

Whatever they cost, they will pay for themselves in the first season. Paraffin has replaced the brandy-soaked writing paper and layers of cotton batting once used to prevent molding [*note*: paraffin in no longer recommended]. The water-bath canner, itself an improvement over more cumbersome pots and boiling-water methods, has been superseded by the steam canner in my kitchen; it not only reduces the amount of water and fuel needed but saves time, too. The steam juicer has eliminated the need for using the traditional jelly bag for extracting juice, though the latter works perfectly well and is less expensive.

With improvements in preserving equipment, less sugar is needed to keep fruit products sound; old-fashioned preserving tended to be lavish in its use of sweeteners. Perhaps surprisingly, the freezer has only a limited role in preserving fruit. Why reap the benefits of sun-ripened fruit and then store that fruit in a freezer for an unlimited time when simple techniques will not only suffice but also produce a better product? Canned blueberries vacuum sealed at their best will keep a long time if stored in a cool place away from light and heat; they will be just as delicious as when they were first packed and sealed in their own juices.

All the fruits described in *The Old-Fashioned Fruit Garden,* except, of course, the wild fruits, were grown on less than half an acre of land in poor northern soil. I have selected small fruits—strawberries, raspberries, red and black currants, gooseberries, elderberries, and citron, as well as rhubarb—because these do well almost anywhere, are easy for the novice to grow, and are sometimes overlooked. Tree-fruit cultivation is more demanding of soil, climate, and space than small-fruit cultivation. As there are already many excellent books and pamphlets on the subject, I have limited myself to uncommon preserving and cooking recipes in the chapter on wild and tree fruits. If you live in a warmer climate, there are many more fruits, such as figs, cherries, and grapes, that could be included in a small garden. But no matter what fruits you choose to grow, if you intend to have an old-fashioned fruit garden, you must follow the principles of energy efficiency that begin with the way the soil is prepared for planting and continue through to the last step of processing.

The chapters deal with one fruit each, and they are arranged in the order the fruits are harvested, beginning with rhubarb and ending with citron; the chapter on wild and tree fruits follows. I chose to devote individual chapters to each member of the genus *Ribes*—red currants, gooseberries, and black currants. All three have been out of favor for decades, partly because they are host to a fungus called white-pine blister rust, which kills white pines but does not damage the carriers. For most of this century, there have been restrictions against those fruits in the United States; since 1966, with the lifting of a federal ban, each state has regulated their sale. There have been no similar regulations in Canada.

In some states, laws have either been relaxed or not enforced for two reasons: the white pine has declined in commercial value, and the regulations have been ineffective, as *Ribes* species grow abundantly in the wild. Nevertheless, the black currant, which often shoulders all the blame for the disease, continues to be maligned as a result of a general lack of knowledge about its special qualities. It is about time someone in North America rescued this fruit from oblivion. I hope that interested gardeners in the United States will demand a reappraisal of this fruit from the state agencies that are charged with regulating its growth. Perhaps plant breeders and nurserymen will then take up the challenge to make this fruit safe for all to grow, available to everyone who wishes to include it in his garden. There are indications that this is beginning to happen, with more breeding programs being conducted at agricultural research stations and by private researchers.

I have not, however, included a chapter on Josta, a gooseberry-black currant hybrid. Hardy and disease resistant, the Josta was bred in Germany. Its bush is tall and tolerates a wide variety of soil conditions, producing dense clusters of deep-purple berries that can be eaten fresh. Josta bushes are available in Canada and the United States (see Appendix). Although reports are mixed, Josta is worth a try, and suggests more possibilities. Use in similar ways to gooseberries or black currants.

In each chapter, there are guidelines for planting, cultivating, and harvesting the fruit. These are general and meant as a guide, not a blueprint. More detailed directions for fruit growing suitable to your area can be obtained, usually in pamphlet form, from your local cooperative extension office or department of agriculture. You will also learn the fruit varieties appropriate for your area and the ways to deal with your particular environment.

The recipes in this book represent our favorite ways to use fruit, both fresh and processed, the result of years of preserving; some recipes are adaptations of ones in books, and these sources are cited in the bibliography. Each preserving recipe is arranged to coincide with the ripeness of the fruit as it is harvested. Jelly recipes that call for a mixture of ripe and underripe berries precede recipes for juice or wine, where the ripest, juiciest berries are required. Every once in a while, I have inserted accompaniments within the preserving recipes. Black currant jelly, for instance, goes great with cream cheese, so the two recipes appear together. Following the preserving recipes in each chapter, there are "cooking" recipes. In addition, one chapter focuses on basic recipes that allow for the substitution of different fruits. No more frantic searching through cookbooks, with sticky fingers, to find another way to use your bumper crop of strawberries or black currants.

I do not deny that planting, harvesting, and processing an old-fashioned fruit garden is a labor, but I think that once you have tasted your own red currant sauce on your morning pancakes, eaten a bowl of fresh-fruit ice cream, or made what everyone is bound to consider the world's best strawberry jam, you will feel well rewarded. Even spending a day or two picking the fully laden black currant bushes, if you are lucky enough to be able to buy them, can be a respite from more worldly activities. You may also gain much satisfaction from rediscovering the virtues of simplicity. That's a lot to get from a small fruit garden.

THE
Old-
Fashioned
FRUIT
GARDEN

Berry juice

A Short Course in Fruit Preserving

I really didn't know how to boil an egg when I got married in the early 1950s. I certainly knew nothing about fruit preserving. All our fruit products—and all our fruit, for that matter—came straight from the supermarket.

With a growing family and a limited income, however, I learned quickly. Necessity is a good teacher. My husband, Jigs, was the leader in the preserving operation because he had had some experience. It was not long, though, before I understood terms such as *boiling-water bath* and *snap lids*. By the time I was left in sole command, as a result of our expanded farming, I had to contend with a large fruit garden and no help at all.

Not only that. As a full partner in the farm, I spent as much if not more time in the field as in the kitchen. At the height of our fruit season, I could be found making square tonloads of hay on our horse-drawn wagon.

Under such conditions, I streamlined our fruit preserving, the benefits of which I pass on to you. The technology I use remains, with few exceptions, simple, a testimony to the truth I learned some time ago: there is no correlation between using high technology and producing high quality. In fact, technology often gets in the way.

Equipment

When making jam, jelly, or sass, use a 2-gallon (8-L) wide-mouth stainless steel pot. The wide mouth allows for fast evaporation, which makes for quick-setting products. Stainless-steel pots also cook evenly, so they are worth the extra expense. Large wide-mouth enamel preserving pots are good for making preserves, juices, and cooking fruit for drying, all of which call for large batches. Tin or copper pots are not recommended because they discolor and flavor fruit products; aluminum pots are too thin. Other necessities for fruit preserving are a large enamel water-bath canner which comes with a rack and a tight-fitting cover, or a steam canner; 1-qt (1-L), 1-pt (500-mL), and 1/2-pt (250-mL) canning jars and small jelly jars with matching snap lids and screw bands; cheesecloth for a jelly bag, or a steam juicer. *Note: old-timers were the great recyclers, using any jar that will take new snap lids and old screw bands, and re-using vacuum-sealed jars. But this practice, like others (sealing with hot paraffin, sealing jams, jellies, syrups, etc. without processing), is not regarded as safe.* Other utensils include wooden spoons, a small metal spoon, a potato masher, wooden stamper, or chopper (I use an old-fashioned egg chopper) for preparing fruit for jam-making, a jar lifter and kitchen tongs, large screens, trays, and cookie sheets, a long-handled ladle and fork, a food mill, and a wide-mouth funnel.

Terms and Methods

Do not be intimidated by these terms and the descriptions of methods. Considering they provide you with the key to mastering home fruit preserving, they are worth reading carefully.

BOILING-WATER BATH A method of processing homemade fruit products in a water-bath canner so that they do not spoil, that is, become moldy or ferment. *It is now recommended that all homemade fruit products should be processed in a boiling-water bath.* Before processing, seal filled canning jars with snap lids and screw bands. Be sure to wipe the sealing edge of the jar to remove any debris that might cause an imperfect seal, then set the snap lid in place, and screw on the metal band, tightening it all the way.

Always process a full load of jars at a time, using water-filled jars to fill the empty spaces. Place bottled-and-sealed fruits on a rack and then lower the rack into the water-bath canner, partly filled with hot water. Add extra water as necessary, to bring the water level to 1 to 2 inches (2.5 to 5 cm) above the tops of the jars. Also make sure that there is about 1 inch (2.5 cm) of space between the jars to allow the water to circulate. Cover the pot and bring the water to a rolling boil. Count the processing time from this moment. At the end of the processing time, wait 5 minutes before removing cover. Lift the jars out of the water with a jar lifter and cool them on a rack or towel in a draft-free place.

Check canning jars in 12 to 24 hours after processing to make sure they are vacuum sealed. After processing, as the jars are cooling, the lids will be sucked down and become concave and will *snap,* making a vacuum seal. If the lids fail to snap, they will remain convex, and these preserves should be reprocessed or refrigerated and used immediately. After 24 hours, the screw bands can be removed and reused.

The **steam canner**, not to be confused with the pressure canner, is a luxurious alternative to the more traditional boiling-water bath. Follow the manufacturer's directions. These usually specify putting 2 qt (2 L) water in the bottom part of the steam canner and counting the processing time from when steam starts coming out of two holes at the base of the cover.

One benefit of the steam canner is that you can process as little as 1 pt (500 ml) at a time. Another is that it doesn't require nearly as much water as a boiling water bath. Having lived with water scarcity for so many years, the steam canner was a blessing. Directions may call for screw bands to be not fully tightened before processing. Steam canners are more commonly used in Europe, though they are available (see Appendix).

COLD PACK A term for filling canning jars with raw fruit that is then covered with boiling water or syrup. Then the jars are processed in a boiling-water bath or steam canner. The cold-pack method works best with soft fruits like raspberries, which lose their shape when precooked.

EXTRACTION A procedure for cooking fruit in order to extract its juices. To make an extraction, mash the fruit, add water or not, cook it until tender, and strain through a jelly bag. The **steam juicer,** also commonly used in Europe, has eliminated the more time-consuming process of making an extraction. Nonetheless, steam juicers should be reserved for making large quantities. Place the fruit in the top part of the pot. On heating, juice collects in the bottom, ready for jarring or for use in jelly making. Steam juicers are available (see Appendix), but they are rather expensive.

HEADROOM The amount of air left between the top of the canned fruit and the lid. Follow directions, but do not worry excessively about this. The fruit inevitably settles, so allow for this when filling jars.

HOT PACK A term for filling canning jars with precooked hot fruit. I prefer this method to the cold-pack one. Precooked fruit, unlike raw fruit, does not shrink when it is processed in a boiling-water bath. A half-filled jar of preserves is a sorry sight, and the preserves may not keep well.

JELLY BAG A sack for straining fruit when making an extraction. Jelly bags can be made from any porous material, but one of the best is cheesecloth. Buy about 1 yd (1 m) of fine cheesecloth and cut a double layer large enough to be draped in the pot receiving the juice. Using clothespins, secure the material around the lip of the pot and then pour the cooked fruit into the cheesecloth. Gather the four corners of the cheesecloth into pairs of two and tie them together to make a bag that can be suspended from any pole, hook, or nail. Place the receiving pot underneath to catch the dripping juice.

PECTIN The substance in fruits that causes them to jell when combined and cooked with sugar. The amount of pectin in fruits varies: elderberries and rhubarb are low in pectin; strawberries, medium; raspberries, a little higher on the scale; currants, gooseberries, apples, and quince very high. Slightly underripe fruit has more pectin than fully ripe fruit: the substance declines in strength as the fruit ripens and decomposes. Citrus fruits, high in pectin, are added to other marmalades to help them jell as well as give them a piquant taste. Commercial pectins are made from citrus fruit. Traditional pectins, in either crystal or liquid form, require a certain amount of sugar to work (usually a lot). Low-sugar or no sugar-needed pectin requires the addition of unsweetened fruit juice. Instant pectin is for making no-cook jam that must be stored in the freezer (freezer jam).

SCALDED JARS Sterilized jars. Hot scalded jars should always be ready to receive the cooked fruit. First, wash the jars and lids in hot, soapy water and rinse them well. Submerge as many jars as possible into a deep pot of hot, almost boiling water; put the lids in a smaller, shallow pot of hot water. Allow them to simmer until they are ready to be filled. Spear each jar with a long-handled fork and drain over the pot as it is being removed from the water. If you are handy with the fork, you can retrieve the lids the same way. Otherwise, use kitchen tongs.

SHEETS OFF A SPOON A killer for the beginner. When the jelly or jam has cooked at a rolling boil for about 10 minutes or less, begin testing for the jelling point—that is, the point at which the mixture begins to hold its shape when cooled. Use a metal kitchen spoon, not a wooden one, for this test.

Scoop a little of the hot jelly or jam onto the spoon, cool it quickly by

A selection of preserves

blowing across it, then slowly pour the mixture back into the pot, pouring from the *side* of the spoon. If it runs off as water, the mixture is far from ready; if it runs off in two drops, it is as thick as syrup and is close to done; if the two drops have merged and the mixture wrinkles slightly and slides as a whole off the side of the spoon, the jelling point has been reached. Jelly slides and sheets; jam tends to fall in globs. Once you are experienced, you will be able to spot the jelling point of jelly by the look of the boiling mixture: thick and light-colored foaming bubbles.

Steps for Canning and Preserving

The following are general guidelines for understanding the basic procedures involved in making various commonly used fruit products. Once you understand them, you will be able to amend and adapt recipes to suit your situation. In the meantime, consult the preserving recipes I offer, as the details may differ from these descriptions. In addition, you'll find other treasures not discussed here—marmalade, wine, chutney, and butter, for example—because they are more complicated, vary more from recipe to recipe, or are less common.

Here I must also say a few words about the substitution of honey for sugar in fruit preserving. Honey does not combine well with natural pectin and for that reason should not be used in jam or jelly making if a firm set is desired. Furthermore, honey, with its distinctive taste, tends to mask fruit flavors. Sugar, on the other hand, used here in the minimum amounts required for setting, brings out and enhances fruit flavors. Honey, though, does combine well with liquid, so it could be added to juices or to syrups used for preserving whole fruits. Let your preference be your guide.

Jelly

Jelly is made from juice extracted from mashed and heated berries that are cooked with sugar. The jelled mixture should be clear, bright in color, and firm yet tender enough to spread easily on bread. Undercooked jelly is runny, and it becomes moldy. Overcooked jelly is tough, treacly, and strong tasting. The secret of superior jelly lies in using fruits high in natural pectin so that an excessive amount of sugar is not needed for setting. Remember, the faster the jelly or jam sets, the more the fruit flavor is retained, so cook *small* batches in a *large* pot. Note: freezer stored fruit works well for jelly-making.

Steps: Sort berries. Use a combination of about two-thirds of ripe berries and one-third of underripe. (Imperfect berries are okay as long as there is no decay.) Rinse quickly in cold water. Avoid over-handling. Drain.

Place fruit in a large preserving pot, mash with a wooden stamper, and add water if necessary. (Strawberries and raspberries need little or no water; gooseberries and currants may be almost covered with water. The amount added will determine the strength of the juice, and the more concentrated it is, the quicker it will jell.)

Cover pot and simmer fruit until juice runs freely, stirring occasionally to prevent sticking.

Strain hot mixture through a jelly bag [p. 6] and let drip for several hours or overnight. Squeeze bag gently.

Measure juice and cook 4 cups (1 L) at a time in a large stainless-steel pot.

Bring to a boil, covered. Stir in sugar with a long-handled wooden spoon. Add equal amount of sugar to juice. If fruit is high in pectin, use 3/4 cup (175 mL) sugar to each cup (250 mL) juice.

Bring to a boil again. Boil, uncovered, for about 10 minutes, skimming froth as necessary. *If the mixture threatens to boil over, toss a small piece of butter into the pot.*

Begin testing for jelling point. When a small amount of mixture sheets off a metal spoon [p. 6-7], remove from heat.

Let jelly subside, stir, and skim if desired. Pour into hot scalded jelly jars [p. 6], leaving 1/4 inch (5 mm) headroom, wipe jar edges, and seal at once with snap lids and screw bands. Process for 10 minutes in a boiling-water bath or steam canner, or according to recipe. Wait 5 minutes until removing the pot or steam canner cover. Store sealed jars in a cool, dark, dry place.

Note: If jelling point is not reached after 20 minutes of rapid boiling, *stop* cooking, remove pot from heat, and pour mixture into hot scalded jars to use as sass (facing page).

Yield: 2 qt (2 L) fruit makes about four 1/2-pt (250-mL) jars.

Jam

Jam is mashed, partially mashed, or chopped whole fruit cooked with sugar until the mixture thickens—it should spread on a piece of bread without dribbling over the edges. Superior jam has a fresh-fruit flavor, is not overly sweet, is a bit chunky in texture and, of course, has a beautiful bright color. To achieve such a product every time, cook the fruit as soon as possible after it has been picked, include a healthy sprinkling of underripe fruit in the harvest to ensure quick setting, and cook the fruit in small batches in a large pot. Note: freezer stored fruit works very well for jam-making if the fruit was picked in prime condition and quickly frozen.

Steps: Sort fruit. Use a combination of two-thirds of ripe berries and one-third of underripe. Imperfect, bruised berries are okay as long as there is no decay. Rinse berries quickly in cold water. Avoid overhandling. Drain.

Measure 1 qt (1 L) fruit and place in a large stainless-steel pot. *Partially* mash berries with a potato masher or wooden stamper, and coarsely chop strawberries or other fruit, to make a chunkier jam. If berries are tough—such as black currants and gooseberries—add a little water or as directed.

Cover and bring berries to simmering point, stirring once or twice to prevent sticking. Stir in sugar with a long-handled wooden spoon. If not following a recipe, add equal amount of sugar to fruit. If fruit is high in pectin, use 3/4 cup (175 mL) sugar to 1 cup (250 mL) fruit.

Bring mixture to a rolling boil. Stirring occasionally, boil rapidly, uncovered, for no more than 10-15 minutes or until mixture thickens and begins to cling slightly to bottom of pot. A small amount should fall in a glob off the side of a metal spoon (see Sheets Off a Spoon, p. 6-7). If mixture threatens to boil over toss in a small piece of butter.

Remove jam from heat. Let subside, stir, and skim if desired. Pour into hot scalded [p. 6] 1/2-pt (250-mL) or 1-pt (500-mL) jars, leaving 1/4 inch (5 mm) headroom, wipe jar edges, and seal at once with snap lids and screw bands. Process in a boiling-water bath or steam canner for 15 minutes or according to recipe. Wait 5 minutes before removing cover. Store sealed jars in a cool, dark, dry place.

Yield: 1 qt (1 L) fruit makes 1 1 /2 to 2 pt (750 mL to 1 L) jam.

Sass

I will be frank. *Sass,* a New England colloquial term for all the vegetables in the garden (from "garden sass" or "sauce") was in the beginning, nothing more than failed jam or jelly, which, I and a zillion other cooks discovered, makes fine toppings for pancakes, ice cream, etc. To make sass on purpose, use any jam or jelly recipe, reduce the amount of sugar, and cook the mixture until it only thickens, not jells. Sass making is great for beginners: it is a foolproof process. There is no need to cook in small batches, no need to know the crucial jelling point, and the result is always delicious.

Steps: Sort and wash fruit as for jam [p. 9]. (Some recipes call for ripe fruit, allowing for overripe or damaged fruit as well.)

In a large stainless-steel pot, partially mash 2 qt (2 L) berries. Cover and bring to simmering point, stirring as necessary. Or make an extraction [p. 5] as for jelly, bringing 2 qt (2 L) juice to a boil, covered.

Stir in sugar. If following a jam or jelly recipe, use one-half to three-quarters the amount called for. Bring mixture to a boil and boil, uncovered, for 10 to 20 minutes or until mixture thickens.

Remove sass from heat and let subside. Stir. Pour into hot scalded jars [p. 6], leaving about 1/2 inch (1 cm) headroom, wipe jar edges, and seal at once with snap lids and screw bands. Process canning jars in a boiling-water bath [p. 4] or steam canner for 20 minutes or according to recipe. Wait 5 minutes before removing cover. Store sealed jars in a cool, dark, dry place.

Yield: *2* qt (2 L) fruit or juice makes about 4 pt (2 L) sass.

Preserves

Preserves are whole fruit preserved in a sugar or honey syrup. They need not be nearly so sweet as the store-bought variety. Home preserves are just sweet enough to bring out the natural fruit flavor. They can be eaten straight out of the jar or with cream; they can be poured over cakes, mixed with different fruits; their juice can be used for gelatin.

Steps: Sort fruit. Use perfectly ripe, *not* overripe, fruit. Rinse quickly in cold water. Drain.

Follow one of these procedures:

(a) Layer fruit and sugar (1/2 to 1 cup/125 to 250 mL sugar to each qt/L fruit) consecutively in a large preserving pot. Cover and let stand for several hours or overnight to draw out juices. Slowly bring mixture to a boil, stirring as necessary to prevent sticking.

(b) In a large preserving pot, add sugar to fruit, cover, and heat until simmering, stirring as necessary.

(c) In a large stainless-steel pot, make a syrup of 2 or 3 cups (500 or 750 mL) sugar to 1 qt (1 L) water. If using 2 qt (2 L) fruit or less, add fruit to syrup. Otherwise, add syrup to fruit in a large preserving pot. Bring to simmering point, stirring as necessary.

Remove preserves from heat. Ladle into hot scalded jars [p. 6], leaving 1/2 inch (1cm) headroom, wipe jar edges, and seal at once with snap lids and screw bands. Process in a boiling-water bath or steam canner for 20 minutes or according to recipe. Wait

5 minutes before removing cover. Store sealed jars in a cool, dark, dry place.

Note: To can fruit without sugar, precook fruit in a little water, ladle into hot scalded jars with boiling water, adjust lids, and process for 15 minutes in a boiling-water bath or steam canner.

To can fruit with honey, substitute honey for half the sugar called for in the recipe. Use scant measure or 1/4 cup (50 mL) less honey than half the amount of sugar.

Yield: 2 to 3 lb (1 to 1.5 kg) fruit makes 1 qt (1 L) processed; 1/2 to 1 cup (125 to 250 ml) sugar syrup covers 1 qt (1 L) fruit.

Dried Berries

It is not necessary to have any special equipment for drying fruit, whether drying berries or making apple rings or fruit leathers, although I have seen dandy home-rigged dehydrators (commercial ones make a lot of noise and usually dry only a small amount at a time). Why use electricity when summer sun, air drying, or the heat left over from baking will do just fine? Berries can be dried in the sun, but those simmered first in a sugar or honey syrup keep their flavor, color, and shape better. The syrup can then be bottled and used as a base for juice or sauce. Eat dried berries as they are or use them in baking.

Steps: Sort berries. Use only firm, ripe, less-seedy berries such as black currants, blueberries, or elderberries. Rinse quickly in cold water. Drain.

Using 3 cups (750 mL) fruit to 1 cup (250 mL) sugar or 3/4 cup (175 mL) honey, layer berries and sugar consecutively in a large preserving pot. Cover and let stand overnight to draw out juices.

Bring mixture to a boil, reduce heat, and simmer for 15 minutes, stirring occasionally to prevent sticking.

Remove from heat. Skim out berries or pour mixture through a strainer. Reserve juice.

Put berries on paper-lined trays—heavy brown shopping bags work well. Using a long-handled fork, spread out berries evenly.

Place trays in direct sunlight. If insects are a problem, cover berries with a single layer of cheesecloth.

The next day, change paper, stir berries, and continue stirring daily until they are as dry as raisins, about 3 to 4 days in good sun. Store berries in glass jars or crocks; they will keep almost indefinitely.

Variation: To make juice as a by-product, place reserved juice back on stove. Bring to a boil and pour into hot scalded jars [p. 6], leaving 1/2 inch (1 cm) headroom, and seal at once with snap lids and screw bands. Process 15 minutes or according to recipe. When serving, dilute with water to taste.

Yield: 2 qt (2 L) berries makes about 1 qt (1 L) dried.

Juice

Juice is one of the easiest ways to store an abundant harvest of overripe fruit. Homemade juice is superior to commercial varieties in every way, in fresh-fruit flavor especially. And many kinds of juice are difficult if not impossible to find on the market. Also, homemade juice is useful for making gelatin, adding to punch, and flavoring frosting, ice cream, sorbets and ices. When serving as a drink, dilute it with water to taste.

Steps: Sort fruit. Rinse quickly in cold water. Drain.

In a large preserving pot, combine fruit and water, using 1/2 cup (125 mL) water to each qt (L) fruit. Make an extraction [p. 5] as for jelly. Measure juice.

Bring juice to a boil, covered. If no particular recipe is used, stir in 1/2 cup (125 mL) sugar (or a little less honey) to every qt (L) juice. Bring juice to a boil again, reduce heat, and simmer, uncovered, for 5 minutes.

Remove juice from heat. Pour into hot scalded jars [p. 6], leaving 1/2 inch (1 cm) headroom, wipe jar edges, and seal at once with snap lids and screw bands. Process canning jars in a boiling-water bath [p. 4] or steam canner for 15 minutes or according to recipe. Store sealed jars in a cool, dark, dry place.

Yield: 2 to 3 qt (2 to 3 L) fruit makes 1 qt (1 L) juice.

Leather

Talk about simple technology! You may want to buy a wood-burning cookstove just to make leather, although a just warm gas or electric oven will work, too. I dry my leathers in a just-warm oven after baking, on the surface of the stove away from the heat, or underneath the stove, a source of steady warmth as any cat will tell you. As a result, I am able to turn literally bushels of fruit into a delicious, natural confection. Any fruit can be used—soft fruits, leftovers, odd bits and pieces at the end of the season. This is a good way to use fruit too good to discard but unsuitable for processing or eating fresh. All sorts of combinations are possible, too: raspberry and strawberry; red currant and gooseberry; raspberry and red currant; apple and cranberry, blueberry, pear, peach, or plum. Pulp the fruit, spread it thinly in a pan, and dry it completely. The finished product is chewy and tasty. Also, use leathers in fruit dishes: just cut them into small pieces and soak them in water. Below are general steps; directions may differ according to individual recipes.

Steps: Chop or mash fruit to a pulp, removing seeds and pits. Use a blender, if desired, to make a smooth purée. For hard fruits, cut up and place in a large preserving pot. Add a little water and bring fruit to a boil. Simmer until soft, adding sugar or honey to taste if desired, then put fruit through a food mill.

Spread pulp evenly about 1/8 to 1/4 inch (3 to 5 mm) thick on cookie sheets lined with heavy plastic wrap—cut-up freezer bags work well.

Set trays in oven after heat has been turned off or at a temperature of 120° to 140°F (50° to 60°C). Leave oven door open partway.

After several days, when leather is dry on top, lift it carefully from plastic. Remove plastic and turn leather over to dry other side. Set trays back in oven until leather feels as dry and as pliable as its namesake. (You can also dry it until brittle. Both are usable.)

When cool, roll up large pieces of leather in a plastic bag and store in a large jar or crock. If leather becomes damp, remove lids. (To store brittle leather, break it into small pieces and place in jars, crocks, or plastic bags. In plastic bags, it will soften a bit.) True leather will keep for years. Our apple leather, still good, is over twenty years old. You can appreciate how jerky, a sort of dried meat leather from raw, marinated meat, was once such a reliable source of sustenance on the frontier.

Yield: 1 1/2 to 2 1/2 lb (750 g to 1.25 kg) fruit makes two average-sized cookie sheets of leather.

Rhubarb

Rhubarb and the small fruits are the backbone of the home fruit garden. All are hardy, all are easy to grow under a wide range of conditions, all are productive in a small area, and almost all survive some neglect. Rhubarb, though strictly speaking a perennial vegetable, is the first fruit we harvest. We look forward to it in the early spring, watching the ground closely for some signs of the emerging tips that will become the first stalks, the most tender of the new season. Processed fruit is fine for the winter, but in late May, when the pile of stored cabbages gives out and the apple bin is empty, we hanker for something truly fresh. No doubt we could rush the rhubarb season by covering a plant or two with plastic to warm the ground and speed the growth of stalks, but we prefer to let nature take its course.

We could not think of any fruit garden without thinking of at least a half-dozen clumps of rhubarb, for pies and stewing and marmalade and juice all season—at least until midsummer. If you enjoy the special flavor of this old-fashioned fruit, then you must plant at least a few clumps, for it makes only a brief appearance in the marketplace. Just six plants, with their broad leaves, make an attractive and impenetrable hedge in our kitchen garden.

Rhubarb is easy to grow. It needs a southern exposure, good drainage, and plenty of fertilizer (manure or compost) and moisture—ingredients essential to maintaining healthy and abundant leaf growth, the key factor in the production of large, healthy stalks. Rhubarb is especially suited to northern climates. The cold winter gives the plant a season of rest, and then it can put all its energy into stalk production in the spring.

Planting

Rhubarb plants are not hard to find, either at a friend's or at a local nursery. Two plants will, when established, yield plenty of stalks for one person. Most gardeners like to have two types: a red one for its color and a green one for its many uses. Valentine, Ruby, and McDonald are popular varieties, but sometimes, as we do, people have excellent unknown types taken from a neighbor's garden.

Grow plants from pieces taken from the crowns of dormant plants, each piece having two or three buds. (The crown is the nubby part that is above ground and attached to the roots below.) In the northeast, plant rhubarb in the spring to ensure sufficient root growth before cold weather and freezing temperatures set in. In areas where soil drainage is a problem, grow the plants on a slope, preferably one with a southern exposure.

To plant, make holes about the depth of the blade of a shovel and the width of 2 shovelfuls. The holes should be approximately 1 yd (1 m) apart, as the roots will eventually spread that distance laterally. Water the hole and refill it with a shovelful of well-rotted compost and then a layer of topsoil. Set the piece of rhubarb crown into this mixture, making sure the buds are 2 to 3 inches (5 to 7.5 cm) below the soil line. Firmly tamp the soil around the plant and water it. Weed the plant well all summer, and if the weather is dry and windy, surround the new growth with a layer of mulch.

Cultivating

In the second season, after rhubarb shoots have appeared, weed each plant thoroughly. Then fertilize and mulch as follows: spread 3 to 4 shovelfuls of well-rotted compost around the plant, but *do not* cover the crown; cover the compost completely with cardboard, worn-out nonsynthetic carpet, or any nonporous decomposable material; put a fairly thick layer of straw, sawdust, or whatever mulching material is available on top of the paper to hold it down. This fertilizer-mulch not only provides the roots with food for new plants but also helps conserve moisture for the growing leaves and stalks. In time, all the layers will break down to form a friable humus around each plant. The fertilizer-mulch technique is particularly valuable in areas where the soil is poor and the growing conditions are difficult.

In the fall, when the plants are dormant, throw a shovelful of manure over each plant; fresh manure is okay, and if it contains straw, so much the better. In the spring, when new growth begins, this light mulch will give some protection against late frosts and will help promote early harvests by giving extra nourishment to the soil. With the spring fertilizer-mulch and the fall dressing of manure, special winter protection is unnecessary, even in harsh northern climates.

To get early production in the spring, make a little hotbed around each plant. Place a box, open at both ends, over the emerging tips and heap fresh, strawy horse manure around the sides of the box. Also cover the top of the box. Harvest growing stalks through the open sides, but when warmer weather arrives, remove the box and let growth occur naturally. (A piece of plastic draped over the tips and held in place with a few clumps of manure will bring the same results. Remove the plastic as the stalks grow.)

It is important to pull seed stalks whenever you see them. They have white plumelike flowers, and they take away from the plant's ability to produce stems, the only edible parts of rhubarb. They are attractive, though, so if you have a large enough patch, you can leave a few fluffy white blooms for a great distant accent.

Harvesting

Always *pull* rhubarb stalks, never cut them—cutting leaves open wounds that encourage disease. Grasp each stalk near the base of the plant, twist it slightly in one direction, and pull. Cut off the leaves, which contain a poisonous concentration of oxalic acid, and throw them onto the compost heap. We lay them around the rhubarb plants as we harvest the stalks, to discourage weeds and add to the mulch that is already there.

In the northeast, the rhubarb season extends from late May to mid-July, depending on the varieties. Stalks may be lightly harvested from new plants in the second year of growth and for 3 to 5 weeks in the third year. Thereafter, if the plants are healthy, harvesting can continue until stalk production has noticeably slowed down. A good plan is to harvest all the usable stalks (the large ones) from each plant as they are produced, turning them into sundry products. Generally, the all-red variety is tender early in the season but quickly turns stringy; the greenish-red one is good for all-season production; and the all-green large-stalked kind, often found in abandoned farmyard patches, is best harvested late in the season. After harvesting, plants need a one- or two-week rest, depending on local growing conditions, to regrow sufficient stalks for another picking. Remember, each plant should have a good growth of leaves left at the end of the season for future stalk production.

Preserving, Canning, Freezing, and Cooking

When the stalks are still tender, early in the season, it is the best time to start preserving rhubarb. Canned rhubarb is easy. Just layer the cut up fruit with sugar, heat until fruit is tender, then pour into jars and process a short time. Freezing tender rhubarb stalks to use later with strawberries is easy too.

Canned Rhubarb

A MIXTURE OF THE ALL-RED AND GREENISH-RED VARIETIES MAKES AN ATTRACTIVE PRESERVE THAT CAN BE USED IN PIES OR EATEN WITH SWEET CREAM AND CANNED STRAWBERRIES; THE DRAINED JUICE CAN BE USED IN GELATIN.

Makes about 7 qt (7 L)

15 lb rhubarb (7.5 kg)
6 1/2 cups sugar (1.625 L)

Cut early tender stalks into 1-inch (2.5-cm) pieces. For fast cutting, assemble 3 or 4 stalks, lay them flat on a board, and with a sharp knife, karate length of stalks.

Measure cut fruit. Using 1/2 cup (125 mL) sugar to each qt (L) rhubarb, layer fruit and sugar consecutively in a large preserving pot until pot is no more than half full. Cover and let stand for 3 to 4 hours, allowing sugar to draw out juices. Slowly heat mixture to boiling point and boil for 30 seconds, stirring often.

Remove mixture from heat. Ladle into hot scalded canning jars [p. 6], leaving 1/2 inch (1 cm) headroom, and adjust lids. Process 15 minutes in a boiling-water bath [p. 26] or steam canner.

Cut up fruit without sugar, pack it in a bag or freezer container, and freeze until needed. Then it is time for marmalade: just simmer cut-up fruit with sugar and oranges—delicious.

Continue eating bowlfuls of stewed rhubarb and rhubarb pies for as long as you can, but one July day you will know that from then on it is rhubarb-juice time. Good for winter breakfasts, as well as for hot summer days, this juice, made with oranges and lemons, preserves rhubarb flavor in a refreshing way. Rhubarb wine uses end-of-the-season stalks, too. Review Short Course [p. 3–14] before preserving.

Rhubarb Marmalade I

This is an old, unusual recipe adapted from an ancient cookbook, one of the treasures of my collection. Actually, my husband, Jigs, discovered it when searching for a way to preserve hundreds of pounds of rhubarb harvested from an abandoned farmyard patch. With this recipe, you can cook fairly large batches at a time, even stirring with an archetypal long-handled wooden spoon. Use tender stalks.

Makes 7 1/2 pt (3.75 L)

8 juicy oranges
4 lb sugar (2 kg)
5 lb rhubarb (2.5 kg)

Remove peel, in quarters, from oranges and set aside. Divide oranges into sections, removing seeds, and cut sections into small pieces. Place orange pieces in a large preserving pot.

Prepare peel. Put quartered orange peel in a saucepan, cover with cold water, and boil until tender. Drain and cool. Scrape off white part of skin with a small sharp knife (or slither it off in one quick motion). Using kitchen scissors, cut peel into tiny pieces. Set aside.

Cut rhubarb into 1/2-inch (1-cm) pieces; add to orange pieces. Cover fruit, bring to a boil, uncover, and boil for 30 minutes, conscientiously stirring bottom of pot with a long-handled wooden spoon to prevent scorching. Stir in sugar and prepared peel. Cook slowly for about 2 hours or until mixture thickens, stirring as necessary.

Remove marmalade from heat. Stir. Pour into hot scalded jars [p. 6], leaving 1/4 inch (5 mm) headroom, and seal with snap lids and screw bands. Process in a boiling-water bath [p. 26] or steam canner for 10 minutes.

Swisher Family Never-Fail Pie Crust

Mike Swisher's Dutch ancestors settled in Virginia where they were fruit farmers. The success of this unique heirloom recipe (tested in our kitchen) is the combination of a cold paste worked into the cold butter-flour mixture; part lard or shortening works too. For a 2-crust 9-inch (23 cm) pie.

2 cups all-purpose flour, sifted (500 mL)
1 tsp salt (5mL)
¾ cup + 1 Tbsp unsalted butter, chilled (177 mL + 15 mL)
¼ cup water, iced (50 mL)

Reserve 6 T (88 mL) of the flour and mix it with the ice water to make a paste. Blend cold butter with remainder of flour. When blended completely add flour paste and stir with a fork or work in with finger. Work dough only until it coheres—as little as possible. Form into a ball and chill while you make the filling. Cut dough in half and roll out bottom crust. Fill pie, roll out top crust, and bake at 400° F (200° C) for 10 minutes, then at 350° F (180° C) for about 45 minutes or until filling is bubbling.

Roll out any leftover dough and spread with cinnamon and sugar. Roll up and bake in a 400° F (200° C) oven for 5 to 10 minutes or until lightly browned. These are called Rollies in our family and are absolutely delicious.

To make baked pie shells, prick bottom crust and bake at 400° F (200° C) for 15 minutes.

Rhubarb-Strawberry Jam

If you still have tender stalks of rhubarb when your strawberries ripen or froze some tender stalks, try this old-fashioned jam.

Makes about 2 pt (1 L)

1 qt hulled strawberries (1 L)
1 cup water (250 mL)
1 lb rhubarb (500 g)
4 cups sugar (1 L)

In a large stainless-steel pot, lightly mash or chop strawberries. Cut rhubarb into 1/2-inch (1-cm) pieces; add to strawberries. Mix. Add water, cover, and simmer mixture until fruit is soft. Stir in sugar and bring mixture to a rolling boil. Stirring as necessary, boil, uncovered, for about 15 minutes or until mixture thickens and begins to cling to bottom of pot.

Remove jam from heat and let subside. Stir, skimming if desired. Fill hot scalded jars [p. 6] to 1/4 inch (5 mm) from the top and seal at once with snap lids and screw bands. Process in a boiling-water bath [p. 26] or steam canner for 15 minutes.

English Muffins

ONCE YOU HAVE MADE RHUBARB MARMALADE, YOU *MUST* MAKE YOUR OWN ENGLISH MUFFINS. YOU WILL NEVER BUY THEM AGAIN. BEFORE TOASTING THESE MUFFINS, TEAR THEM APART WITH A FORK TO GIVE THEM THEIR CHARACTERISTIC ROUGH TEXTURE. THIS WAY, THEY CAN SOAK UP MORE BUTTER BEFORE THE MARMALADE IS ADDED.

Makes 1 dozen

1/4 tsp ginger (1 mL)
1 tsp salt (5 mL)
1 tsp sugar (5 mL)
1 tsp sugar (5 mL)
1 Tbsp dry yeast (15 mL)
3/4 cup cold water (175 mL)
1/4 cup warm water (50 mL)
4 cups unbleached white flour (1 L)
1/2 cup milk (125 mL)
3 Tbsp shortening (50 mL)
Cornmeal

In a large bowl, sprinkle ginger, 1 tsp (5 mL) sugar, and yeast over warm water to help the yeast dissolve faster, especially in a drafty kitchen! Meanwhile, in a pot, scald milk, melting shortening in it at same time. Stir in salt and 1 tsp (5 mL) sugar. Remove from heat and add cold water, cooling mixture to warm.

Add cooled milk mixture to dissolved yeast. Add 2 cups (500 mL) flour. Mix well. Mix in remaining flour or whatever amount needed to make a bread-like dough that is a bit stickier. Turn dough out onto a lightly floured board and knead until smooth and elastic. Return to bowl and grease top of dough. Cover bowl with a clean towel and place in a warm spot to allow dough to rise.

When dough has doubled in size, punch it down and cut into 12 equal pieces. Roll each piece into a ball. Flattening each piece a bit, dip each one, on all sides, in a bowl of cornmeal. Place muffins on a board sprinkled with cornmeal and let rise slightly.

Heat an ungreased pancake griddle on top of stove. When hot, cook muffins until browned on both sides.

Freezing Rhubarb

With the acquisition of a freezer late in life, I discovered that the tender stalks of the early harvest freeze well for later use with strawberries or other fruits (rhubarb combines well with blueberries) or for stewing or baking. Just cut up as you would for fresh, stewed rhubarb, and place in a zip-lock freezer bag or container. No sugar needed to keep in fresh condition.

Rhubarb Juice

Make this juice with tough, stringy stalks. In winter, pour it over clean fresh snow. In summer, pour it over chipped ice, adding a sprig or two of mint, or use it to flavor and sweeten ice tea (two-thirds tea, one-third juice). Add to punch at any season. When serving, dilute it with water to taste.

Makes about 3 1/2qt (3.5 L)

5 lb rhubarb (2.5 kg)
3 qt water (3 L)
2 lemons
1 1/2 cups sugar (375 mL)
2 oranges

Cut rhubarb into 1-inch (2.5-cm) pieces and cut up oranges and lemons, skin and all. Place fruit in a large preserving pot and add water. Cover and simmer until fruit is soft. Strain through a jelly bag [p. 6] and let drip for several hours or overnight.

Bring juice to a boil, covered, stir in sugar, and bring to a boil again. Boil, uncovered, for 5 minutes.

Remove juice from heat. Pour into hot scalded canning jars [p. 6], leaving 1/2 inch (1 cm) headroom, and adjust lids. Process for 15 minutes in a boiling-water bath [p. 26] or steam canner.

Rhubarb Sherbert

Delicious and refreshing. Review An Assortment of Basics [p. 139–146] for general comments regarding using an ice cream machine.

Makes about 1 1/2 qt (1.5 L)

3 cups unsweetened rhubarb juice (750 mL)
2 cups milk (500 mL)
1 cup sugar (250 mL)

Pre-mix juice, sugar, and milk in ice cream machine canister, cover with freezing cover and chill for faster freezing. When ready to begin freezing, turn on the machine, set canister in ice bucket, pour in water and layer ice and salt as directed. Remove freezing cover, insert paddle, and put mixing cover in place, adding more water according to directions. Turn on machine and add more salt and ice as directed when ice begins to melt. Continue freezing until sorbet is the consistency you want. This should take about 20-25 minutes or less. Remove canister, stir to blend if necessary, store in freezer for an hour or more, then you may remove sherbert to a plastic freezer container and return to freezer.

Rhubarb Wine

IF AGED FOR SEVERAL SEASONS, THIS WINE TASTES LIKE A GOOD SHERRY. TRY IT CHILLED OR WITH CRUSHED ICE. USE TOUGH, STRINGY RHUBARB.

Makes 3 to 4 qt (3 to 4 L)

5 lb rhubarb (2.5 kg)
1 Tbsp wine or baking yeast (25 mL)
1 lemon
1 gallon boiling water (4 L)
3 lb sugar (1.5 kg)

Finely chop clean rhubarb and lemon and place in a 2-gallon (8-L) crock or plastic bucket. Add boiling water and cover. Let stand for 3 days, stirring 3 times a day. Strain and reserve juice.

Dissolve yeast in a little warm water. Add sugar and yeast to juice, stirring in well. Cover mixture and let stand in a warm place for about 1 month.

Siphon wine into 1-gallon (4-L) glass jugs, using wads of cotton batting for stoppers. When wine stops fermenting, or stops bubbling, siphon into 1-qt (1-L) bottles and seal with caps or corks. Store in a cool, dark, dry place. If sealed with corks, store lying down.

Note: One of the best fruit wines, this is a sweet wine until well aged. For a drier wine, reduce sugar to 2 cups (500 mL).

Rhubarb Marmalade II

THIS IS ANOTHER OLD RECIPE, FROM *MY LADYE'S COKE BOOK,* PUBLISHED IN 1924 BY THE BRATTLEBORO, VERMONT, WOMAN'S CLUB. THIS SMALL BOOK COVERS EVERY ASPECT OF COOKING, AS WELL AS HOUSEHOLD HINTS SUCH AS HOW TO USE EGG SHELLS FOR CLEANING BOTTLES, HOW TO MEND KID GLOVES, AND HOW TO MAKE SOAP.

Makes about 1 1/2 pt (750 mL)

2 cups unsweetened stewed rhubarb (500 mL)
1 cup orange juice (250 mL)
4 cups sugar (1 L)
1 cup sliced orange (250 mL)

In a large stainless-steel pot, simmer together fruit and juice, uncovered, for 1 hour. Stir in sugar and continue simmering for about 30 minutes or until mixture thickens.

Remove marmalade from heat. Stir. Pour into hot scalded jars [p. 6], leaving 1/4 inch (5 mm) headroom, and seal at once with snap lids and screw bands. Process in a boiling-water bath [p. 26] or steam canner for 10 minutes.

Rhubarb Bread

THIS IS A QUICK BREAD. USE TENDER STALKS.

3/4 cup honey (175 mL)
1 1/2 cups diced rhubarb (375 mL)
1/2 cup cooking oil (125 mL)
1 egg
1/2 tsp vanilla (2 mL)
1/2 cup chopped nuts or sunflower seeds (125 mL)
1 cup buttermilk (250 mL)
2 cups unbleached white flour (500 mL)
1/2 cup whole wheat flour (125 mL)

Topping:

1/2 cup brown sugar (125 mL)
1 tsp cinnamon (5 mL)
1 tsp salt (5 mL)
1 1/2 Tbsp butter (20 mL)

In a large bowl, mix together honey, oil, and egg; beat well. In a separate bowl, dissolve baking soda in buttermilk and set aside.

Combine white and whole-wheat flours. Add salt. Add flour and buttermilk alternately to honey-oil mixture, stirring after each addition. Stir in rhubarb, vanilla, and nuts or sunflower seeds. Pour batter into a large greased loaf pan or two small ones.

Prepare topping. Mix together brown sugar, cinnamon, and butter in a small bowl. Sprinkle over bread. Bake bread in a 325°F (160°C) oven for about 1 hour or until a sharp knife or cake tester inserted in center comes out clean.

Note: If you do not have buttermilk, mix together 1/2 cup (125 mL) milk and 1/2 cup (125 mL) yogurt or sour cream.

Stewed Rhubarb

RHUBARB SHOULD BE STEWED EARLY IN THE SEASON, BUT IF IT IS STEWED LATE, FOLLOW THE ALTERNATIVE METHOD BELOW.

Serves 4

1 lb rhubarb (500 g)
Sugar

Cut tender stalks into 1-inch (2.5-cm) pieces and place in a stainless-steel pot. Add a little water, cover and, stirring to prevent scorching, boil rhubarb until tender, only a few minutes. Remove from heat. While still warm, add sugar to taste.

Note: An alternative way to make stewed rhubarb is to layer cut-up stalks with sugar, using 1/2 cup (125 mL) sugar to each qt (L) rhubarb. Cover and let stand for 2 hours. Bring to a boil and simmer until fruit is soft, stirring occasionally.

Variation: To make *Rhubarb Fool,* purée stewed rhubarb and mix with sweet cream.

Rhubarb Pie

The egg makes this rhubarb pie a little different, quite rich, but not overly sweet. Use only tender stalks.

2 1/2 cups diced rhubarb (625 mL)
1 egg, beaten
Dash salt
1 cup sugar (250 mL)
Pastry (see below)
2 Tbsp flour (25 mL)

In a large bowl, mix together diced rhubarb, sugar, flour, beaten egg, and salt. Put filling in an unbaked 9-inch (23-cm) pie shell and cover with a top crust. Prick top crust a few times with a fork. Bake pie in a 375°F (190°C) oven for about 50 minutes or until inner juices boil over a bit.

Rhubarb Upside-Down Cake

The orange-cinnamon glaze combines well with the sweetened rhubarb to give this dessert a distinctive flavor. Use tender stalks.

2 heaping cups diced rhubarb (500 mL)
1/2 tsp salt (2 mL)
1/4 cup shortening or lard (50 mL)
2/3 cup sugar (150 mL)
1 Tbsp flour (15 mL)
1 egg, beaten
1 tsp grated orange rind (5 mL)
3 Tbsp milk (50 mL)
1 tsp cinnamon (5 mL)
1 cup flour, sifted (250 mL)

Glaze:

2 Tbsp sugar (25 mL)
2 Tbsp orange juice (25 mL)
2 tsp baking powder (10 mL)
1 Tbsp sugar (15 mL)

Arrange rhubarb in a lightly greased 9-inch (2.5-L) square baking dish. In a bowl, mix together 2/3 cup (150 mL) sugar, 1 Tbsp (15 mL) flour, orange rind, and cinnamon. Sprinkle over rhubarb, stirring lightly with a fork to distribute sugar mixture.

Sift together 1 cup (250 mL) flour, 2 Tbsp (25 mL) sugar, baking powder, and salt. Cut in shortening or lard. Mix in beaten egg and milk. Drop batter by spoonfuls over rhubarb mixture. Bake cake in a 350°F (180°C) oven for 25 minutes.

Meanwhile, prepare glaze. Mix together 2 Tbsp (25 mL) orange juice and 1 Tbsp (15 mL) sugar. Drizzle over baked cake and return to oven for 15 minutes.

Note: To make with canned rhubarb [p. 41], substitute 1 qt (1 L) drained canned rhubarb for fresh and omit 2/3 cup (150 mL) sugar.

Strawberries

Although an aura of romantic nostalgia surrounds the wild North American strawberry, the backyard gardener can be well satisfied with establishing and maintaining a patch of the cultivated type. The cultivated strawberry is a hybrid of two wild species, the American *Fragaria virginiana* and the South American *Fragaria chiloensis,* bred for vigor, large fruit, and disease resistance.

Some insist that wild strawberries have a more intense flavor than the domesticated. But there are so many varieties with differing degrees of sweetness and taste that it does not seem at all compromising to have a splendid patch of cultivated strawberries in one's own backyard, ready to eat fresh with cream, top a shortcake, or turn into jam.

Strawberries were first cultivated in 1840, and it is not surprising that since then they have grown in popularity with home gardeners. Commercial production has increased as well, even though the wild species are uniquely flavored and it is a pleasant pastime to roam favorite meadows and hillsides in search of the small bright-red berries.

There is, of course, one all-important difference to keep in mind: wild strawberries require only picking; cultivated strawberries, on the other hand, require faithful attention. In fact, of all the fruit you are likely to grow in a small fruit garden, strawberries require the most work. Once the essentials of successful production are understood,

however, maintenance, while at times laborious, is not difficult. The reward, a bountiful supply of delicious fruit, is worth the effort.

The essence of sustained high-quality strawberry production can be simply stated: strawberries *must* be weed free. For the gardener, this means getting down on hands and knees in the early spring and pulling out *each* weed from among the plants and between the rows. Otherwise, the roots of the weeds become inextricably intertwined with the many strands of the growing strawberry plant. This is a serious business, one to which you can devote whole days.

If you want your strawberry patch to be more than a one-season affair, the following plan, based on single-row cultivation, not matted-row, is guaranteed to bring good results.

Planting

If the area available for your strawberries is small, stick to one variety; if not, try two to see which one you prefer. There are an endless number of strawberry varieties to choose from among June bearers (the traditional type). Everbearers produce an early and late crop, produce few runners, and can be grown where summer temperatures are consistently in the high range. Day neutral types (true everbearers) are hardier, produce better quality fruit and few runners; plants should be replaced every other year or even every year to maintain high productivity. The everbearing and day neutral strawberries are best for planting in a strawberry jar or space-saving pyramid. Consult your local Cooperative Extension office for detailed information about the best varieties of strawberries for your area (see Appendix for locating the office nearest you). Your choice also depends, of course, on your taste. We prefer the June bearing Bounty for its intensely sweet flavor, but commercial growers don't because this strawberry is not as large as other varieties. In any event, it is best to get plants (consisting of crowns and roots) from local nurseries rather than from a friend, as nursery-grown stock, with its good root system, is cultivated specially for the purpose of starting new plants.

Twenty-five plants are plenty to start with: under reasonable conditions, one plant will produce at least 1 qt (1 L) strawberries. It is important to start small with strawberries. Learn their culture before getting in too deep because there is nothing more discouraging than facing a large bed of weedy strawberries in the spring. Then it's easy to give up and say, "The weeds took over." If you plan sensibly, the weeds will never have a chance.

Choose a well-drained sunny spot for your strawberry bed, either a level area or a slight, not steep, incline. Enrich sandy or clay soil with a lot of organic matter. It's a good idea to cultivate the site a season in advance to help prevent the growth of weeds. Plow or dig the plot by hand in the spring, then work in a good layer of well-rotted compost or manure. The following spring, before planting, smooth the area, making a fine, level surface. Although strawberries are usually planted (and sold) in the spring, an early-fall planting can be successful if there is sufficient moisture to help establish the plants. A dry windy spell means death to new plants.

To plant, hoe rows about 4 to 5 ft (1.25 to 1.5 m) apart. Mark the rows with string, and with a trowel, dig shallow holes about 18 to 24 inches (45 to 60 cm) apart all along the rows. Water each hole, then set in the strawberry plant, spreading out the roots to comfortably fit the space. Firmly tamp the earth around the roots to eliminate air pockets, and make sure the crown of the plant *is exactly* at soil level—correctly set crowns bring hardier, more vigorous plants. While planting, keep the roots of the unplanted strawberry crowns in a bucket of water. If left out in the air, they could easily dry out and wilt.

When all the plants have been set in the ground, lay down a heavy organic mulch between the rows, the second most essential requirement for maintaining high-quality strawberry production. Mulch conserves moisture, helps eliminate weeds, adds nutrients, and improves the texture of the soil. Mulch softens the soil, making spring weeding easier.

We used a mulch made up of two layers of material: a thick nonporous bottom layer of old paper and a 2-inch (5-cm) top layer of eel grass (gathered from Nova Scotia beaches), straw, or rotted sawdust. Eel grass and rotted sawdust also keep slugs away from strawberries during cool, damp weather. With this heavy mulch between the rows, no winter protection was necessary.

If the weather is dry during the week after planting, water the strawberry plants daily until they are established.

Cultivating

Gardeners are usually advised to pick the flowers of first-year strawberry plants to prevent the setting of fruit. The plant, it is believed, needs to put all its energy into maintaining vigorous growth. But it's a matter of choice: we have found that particularly vigorous varieties are not harmed by letting them set fruit the first year. In any case, once the first-year plants are established, in the early spring of their second year, pull out every weed around the plants. (Use a trowel to dig out the roots of the weeds.) Then fill in any spaces left from winter kill with runner plants that have spread in and between the rows. Do not allow the plants in the rows to set more than 2 to 3 runners apiece (simply dig them up), but save some plants to enlarge the patch. This method of cultivation will produce a series of solid narrow rows, much easier to harvest than wide matted rows that have been allowed to fill in with runners. Plants in the single-row method tend to be more vigorous and produce larger berries.

Then there is little to do but wait for the berries and watch for the reappearance of any weeds. Once early-spring weeding has been done and the mulch refurbished or replaced, little weeding is necessary. It is a good idea, though, to root out weeds the first few times you harvest berries. That will probably be sufficient until the end of the season, when you should weed once more.

After the harvest is over, mow the patch, setting the mower blade high to avoid cutting the crowns of the plants. Mowing gets rid of dead leaves and helps rejuvenate the plants by encouraging new leaf growth, essential for maintaining vigorous plants. New growth before the fall gives the plants a better chance of surviving harsh winter conditions.

The third year of growth is the strawberry plant's last season of bearing. For this reason, section your plot into first-, second-, and third-year plants so that there are always strawberry-bearing plants, as well as new replacer plants. Select replacer plants from the extra runners in the established rows. Use only the best-quality plants— the first two runners are considered the best—

young and healthy, with a good root system. Introduce new commercial stock eventually, though, because rows established exclusively with homegrown replacements will "run out"—that is, the plants will decline in vigor and their berries in size. A good plan is to buy new stock every fourth year, after the end of the three-year cycle of every newly established section of the strawberry bed.

Harvesting

In the northeast, the strawberry season usually lasts three weeks, beginning on our farm in early July. When the plants begin to bear heavily, pick strawberries every other day, in the morning. If you pick them while a little underripe—not fully red—store them in a cool basement for 24 hours. At the end of that time, they will be fully ripe and ready to eat fresh or to make into canned preserves. For jam making, pick a mixture of ripe and underripe fruit and use it right away or store in the freezer as directed. When picking, carry two strawberry baskets down each row—one for large perfect berries, the other for culls, or odd-shaped, damaged, or small berries. Fill the perfect-berry box to almost overflowing because the contents will sink slightly. Use up the culls right away and never hull cultivated strawberries until you are ready to use them.

Preserving, Canning, Freezing, And Cooking

The easiest and everyone's favorite way to preserve the essence of strawberries is in jam. Culls make fine jam, but, as already mentioned, use them up right away, for they deteriorate faster than perfect fruit. Canned strawberries are also delicious, and because a lot of berries can be processed at once, canning is a good way to preserve a large quantity of fruit. Do not believe contemporary cookbooks that tell you canned strawberries are not worth doing. Freezing chopped strawberries, mixed with a relatively small amount of sugar, preserves the color and flavor of the fruit, for which there are many uses. Strawberry juice and strawberry sass are luxuries, but why not try them? You can afford to be extravagant with your own strawberry patch—your reward for weeding, and keeping the plants in top condition. More simple but just as satisfying are strawberries and cream. Too often strawberries are gussied up in all sorts of dishes, usually difficult and time consuming to prepare. Having said that, however, I do recommend trying some of the fancier cooking recipes. Review Short Course [p. 3–14] before preserving. And on a warm summer evening, with friends gathered around, why not drop a large, perfect strawberry to soak in everyone's glass of champagne?

The World's Best Strawberry Jam

Strawberry jam is really the reason for this book, because through making it, I discovered the principles of good jam making without added pectin, and fruit preserving in general. Over the years, this jam has been the star of stars, something special to everyone who has tasted it. Yet the recipe is so simple you may question its validity. Harvest ripe and underripe berries and cook them quickly in small batches, and I guarantee a strawberry jam as you have never tasted before.

Makes 1 1/2 pt (750 mL)

4 cups hulled strawberries (1 L)
2 1/2 cups sugar (625 mL)

In a large stainless-steel pot, chop berries enough to produce a chunky, but manageable, spread. Partially thawed frozen and chopped berries work very well. Cover and heat until simmering, stirring as necessary. Stir in sugar and bring to a rolling boil. Stirring occasionally, boil, uncovered, for about 10 minutes or less with prime fruit, until mixture thickens and begins to cling to bottom of pot. This jam should sheet off a metal spoon [p. 6–7].

Remove jam from heat and let subside. Stir, skimming if desired. Fill hot scalded jars [p. 6] to 1/4 inch (5 mm) from the top and seal at once with snap lids and screw bands. Process in the boiling-water bath [p. 26] or steam canner for 15 minutes.

There's no need to tell you how to use strawberry jam, but you may not have thought of trying a spoonful in your morning cereal.

Serves 2 to 3

1 cup medium coarse-ground wheat berries (250 mL)
2 cups hot water (500 mL)
1 scant tsp salt (5 mL)

In a saucepan, stir ground wheat berries into hot water. Add salt, cover, and bring to a boil. Reduce heat and simmer for about 15 to 20 minutes or until all water is absorbed. Ladle into bowls and add jam and cream to taste.

Canned Strawberry Preserves

THESE PRESERVES ARE NOT OVERLY SWEET—GREAT IN A WINTER STRAWBERRY-SHORTCAKE OR IN BAVARIAN CREAM. USE FIRM RIPE WHOLE BERRIES.

Makes 3 1/2 qt (3.5 L)

6 qt hulled strawberries (6 L)
3 cups sugar (750 mL)

In a large preserving pot, layer strawberries and sugar consecutively. Cover and let stand in a cool place for 5 to 6 hours.

Heat mixture slowly, uncovered. Stir occasionally but be careful not to bruise fruit. Bring to boiling point and remove from heat.

Ladle preserves into hot scalded canning jars [p. 6], leaving 1/2 inch (1 cm) headroom, and adjust lids. Process jars in a boiling-water bath [p. 26] or steam canner for 15 minutes.

Freezing Strawberries

Chunky Strawberry Sauce

To make a chunky sauce that can be used to top shortcake, mix with other fruits, canned or frozen, or to stir into yogurt or cereal, cut up hulled fruit and for every 1 qt (1 L) stir in 1/2 cup (125 mL) sugar. I use a hand food processor which is very easy to use, clean, and enables me to process a lot of strawberries in a short time (see Appendix for sources). Leave fruit/sugar mixture at room temperature about 10 minutes to bring out juices. Pour into freezer containers and freeze.

Frozen Whole Strawberries

To freeze whole, hulled strawberries if you're too busy to make them into jam right away, simply put them in a freezer bag. Freezing does not adversely affect their jam making properties.

Strawberry Sass

Many years ago, in New England, "garden sass," a corruption of the English term *garden sauce,* referred to all the vegetables raised in the garden. My family has corrupted the term still further to mean "fruit sauce." Use dead-ripe strawberries, though overripe and damaged ones are fine.

Hulled strawberries
Sugar

In a large preserving pot, simmer strawberries, covered, with a little water. Mash berries and strain through a jelly bag [p. 6]. Let drip for several hours or overnight. Measure juice and cook 2 qt (2 L) at a time in a large stainless-steel pot. Cover, bring to a boil, and stir in 3 cups (750 mL) sugar to each qt (L) juice. Bring to a boil again and cook, uncovered, until desired thickness is reached, about 15 minutes.

Remove sass from heat, let subside, and stir. Pour into hot scalded jars [p. 6], leaving 1/2 inch (1 cm) headroom, and seal at once with snap lids and screw bands. Process in a boiling-water bath [p. 26] or steam canner for 15 minutes.

Strawberry Juice

The flavor and color of this juice is almost unbelievable. Use overripe strawberries, and when serving, dilute with water to taste.

Hulled, mashed strawberries
Sugar or honey

In a large preserving pot, combine strawberries and water, using 1/2 cup (125 mL) water to each qt (L) mashed fruit. Simmer, covered, until juice runs freely and strawberries are tender. Strain through a jelly bag [p. 6] and let drip for several hours or overnight.

Measure juice. Heat, and stir in 1/2 cup (125 mL) sugar (or a little less honey) to every qt (L) juice. Bring to a boil and let boil, uncovered, for 5 minutes.

Remove juice from heat. Pour into hot scalded jars [p. 28], leaving 1/2 inch (1 cm) headroom, and seal at once with snap lids and screw bands. Process in a boiling-water bath [p. 26] or steam canner for 15 minutes.

Strawberry Leather

We learned to make leathers from a wonderful friend in her 80s. She is remarkably thrifty, not to mention active. There is no such thing as wasted produce at her home. Use overripe or damaged fruit as long as the flavor is not impaired.

In a large preserving pot, mash hulled strawberries to a pulp. Spread pulp 1/4 inch (5 mm) thick on cookie sheets lined with heavy plastic wrap. Set pans in sun or in a 120°F (50°C) oven. When pulp is completely dry on one side, about 3 days, turn over and dry other, removing plastic.

When leathers can be lifted off pans in sheets, they are done. Cool leathers on a cake rack, cut into pieces, and store in plastic bags or any covered container. Check containers occasionally for mold. Or dust leathers with icing sugar and stack in layers with wax paper in between.

Strawberries and Cream

We are aficionados of this simple dish and have put a lot of thought and care (though not much work) into its preparation. You can, of course, buy different kinds of cream—sweet, whipping, or sour— and if you are lucky enough to own a cow, preferably a Jersey, "the cream cow," you can make your own first-rate products. But do not just cut up strawberries and serve them with some sort of cream. That's a common dish. Here's our version.

Prepare strawberries. Hull and cut up ripe strawberries and place in a bowl. Sprinkle with a little sugar, cover, and let stand at room temperature for 1 hour to draw out juices.

Prepare sweet cream. Chill fresh milk for at least 24 hours. Skim cream from milk and pour over bowl of prepared strawberries. One gallon (4 L) fresh milk makes about 1 qt (1 L) sweet cream.

Variations: To make *whipping cream,* chill fresh milk for 24 hours. Skim cream from milk. Place cream and a beater in a bowl and chill for several hours. Whip cream and add **a** dollop to a bowl of prepared strawberries.

To make *sour cream,* let sweet cream stand, covered, at room temperature for 24 hours. Add vinegar to taste.

To make *crème fraiche*, stir *whipping cream* into *sour cream* to taste.

Devonshire Cream

Devonshire cream is not actually meant to be eaten with fresh strawberries. Real Devonshire cream is thick enough to spread on hot scones—the way the British eat it—and is lavishly topped with strawberry jam. But if you make your own, either from fresh milk or by thinning cream cheese with sweet cream, you can make it as thick as you choose.

Makes 1 1/2 qt (1.5 L)

Let 2 gallons (8 L) fresh whole milk stand, covered, at room temperature for 6 to 12 hours, depending on how thick and tangy you want cream.

In a large pot, heat milk slowly, uncovered, until surface barely begins to wrinkle. *Do not boil milk; do not stir it while it is heating.*

Remove milk from heat, cover, and chill for 12 to 24 hours, depending on desired thickness. Spoon off thick cream and chill until ready to serve.

While on the subject of dairy products to accompany fruit, it seems like a good time to introduce yogurt, fruit's natural partner. Serve with strawberries or other fruit any way you like. You can't go wrong.

1 qt milk, raw or pasteurized (1 L)
4 Tbsp culture from your preferred yogurt (58 mL)

Heat milk to 180° F (82° degrees C). Let cool to 116° F (47° C). Pour through strainer into an insulated tub (I use a Yogotherm—see Appendix under Cheesemaking Supplies). Stir in culture, stirring well, cover tightly, and leave undisturbed about 4 hours. Remove yogurt container and chill overnight. Alternatively you can stir culture into a little of the cooled milk, then stir this into the rest of the milk, pour through a strainer and stir in as directed.

Greek Yogurt and Yogurt Cheese Spread

Strain yogurt through two thicknesses of cheesecloth until the desired consistency. For Greek-style yogurt, let drain until thicker than regular yogurt but not as thick as yogurt cheese. For cheese, let drain until the consistency of a soft spread. Great with strawberry jam and all jams and jellies.

Strawberry Frosting

FRESH-STRAWBERRY FROSTING IS A NICE WAY TO MARK THE END OF THE HARVEST WHEN JUST A FEW BERRIES WILL GO A LONG WAY. THIS IS ALWAYS A BIG HIT, ESPECIALLY ON A SIMPLE CAKE.

Frosts 1 medixum-sized cake
1/4 tsp salt (1 mL)
1 tsp vanilla (5 mL)
3 Tbsp butter (50 mL)
2 1/2 cups sifted icing sugar (625 mL)
1/4 cup crushed ripe strawberries (50 mL)
Halved perfect strawberries

In a large bowl, blend together salt and butter. In a separate bowl, combine crushed strawberries and vanilla. Add icing sugar and crushed berries alternately to butter. Stir after each addition. Add only enough berries to achieve desired consistency.

Spread frosting over top and sides of cake. Garnish with halved perfect strawberries and let stand for several hours.

Note: In winter, substitute strawberry juice [p. 56] or 1 to 2 Tbsp (15 to 25 mL) strawberry preserves [p. 54–55] for fresh berries.

Two-Egg Cake

THIS IS A GOOD CHOICE FOR STRAWBERRY FROSTING. ALSO USE IT AS A BASE FOR STRAWBERRY SHORTCAKE.

2 cups sifted cake flour (500 mL)
1 tsp vanilla or other flavoring (5 mL)
2 1/2 tsp baking powder (22 mL)
1/4 tsp salt (1 mL)
2 eggs, separated
1/2 cup shortening (125 mL)
2/3 cup milk (150 mL)
3/4 to 1 cup sugar (275 to 250 mL)

Sift together flour, baking powder, and salt. In a bowl, cream shortening. Beat in sugar, and cream until fluffy. Add vanilla.

In a small bowl, beat egg yolks well; beat into shortening mixture. Add flour and milk alternately to shortening-egg mixture, beating smooth after each addition.

In a separate bowl, beat egg whites until stiff; fold into cake batter. Pour batter into a greased 8-inch x 12-inch (3-L) cake pan or standard angel-food cake pan. Bake in a 350°F (180°C) oven for about 50 minutes.

Note: To assemble strawberry shortcake, cut cake into squares and split each square in half. Ladle desired strawberry topping onto bottom layer. Cover with other piece of cake and garnish with more strawberry mixture and with whipped cream [p. 58].

Strawberry Tart

1 qt ripe strawberries (1 L)
2 to 4 Tbsp flour or cornstarch (25 to 75 mL)
1 cup sugar (250 mL)
1/4 tsp salt (5 mL)
1 1/4 cups cold water (300 mL)
1 Tbsp lemon juice (optional) (15 mL)
Baked pie shell [p. 46]
Whipped cream [p. 58]

Hull strawberries, setting aside some for garnish. Cut up remaining berries, place in a pot, and stir in sugar, salt, and lemon juice. In a bowl, dissolve flour or cornstarch in cold water; add to strawberries. Stirring well, bring mixture to a boil, reduce heat, and simmer until thick. Remove from heat, cool, stirring occasionally, and chill.

Pour chilled filling into a baked 9-inch (23-cm) pie shell or 6 baked tart shells and top with whipped cream. Garnish with whole perfect strawberries.

Strawberry Bavarian Cream

Hull strawberries and set aside a handful of perfect ones for decorating. In a bowl, lightly mash remaining strawberries and stir in sugar. Cover and let stand at room temperature for 1 hour.

Serves 6

1 qt ripe strawberries (1 L)
1/2 cup boiling water (125 mL)
3/4 cup sugar (175 mL)
2 cups whipping cream [p. 58] (500 mL)
2 Tbsp gelatin (25 mL)
1/4 cup cold water or strawberry preserves juice [p. 56] (50 mL)

Meanwhile, in a saucepan, sprinkle gelatin over cold water or preserves juice; let stand for 5 minutes. Stir to dissolve gelatin. Add boiling water and heat mixture over low heat, stirring until all gelatin granules are dissolved. Cool, stir in crushed fruit, and chill until jelled.

In a bowl, whip cream; fold into chilled gelatin-strawberry mixture. Pour Bavarian cream into a cold wet mold, bread pan, or individual custard cups. Garnish with a handful of strawberries, whole or halved, and chill for several hours or until firm.

Note: To make with strawberry preserves [p. 54–55], substitute 1 qt(1 L) drained preserves for fresh strawberries and omit sugar.

To make Bavarian-cream tarts, pour chilled Bavarian cream into 6 baked tart shells or small baked pie shells [p. 46]. Garnish with fresh fruit and serve.

Viennese Chocolate Torte

Recommended for fans of Old World confections, this dessert is outrageous. Save it for a big celebration, forget about calories and expense, and glory in the mixture of fruit and chocolate.

6-oz pkg semisweet chocolate chips or bits (175 g)
1/2 pt heavy cream, whipped (p. 57) (250 mL)
4 eggs, separated
1/3 cup sugar (75 mL)
1/3 cup grated nuts (75 mL)

Frosting:

Sweetened crushed strawberries or strawberry jam [p. 54]
6 sq semisweet chocolate
1/2 cup butter (125 mL)

In the top of a double boiler, melt chocolate chips over boiling water; let cool. Meanwhile, in a bowl, beat together egg yolks and sugar. *Beat!* Add nuts and melted chocolate chips.

In a separate bowl, beat egg whites until stiff. *Stiff!* Fold into chocolate mixture. Pour batter into a greased 9-inch (2.5-L) spring-form pan. Bake in a 325°F (160°C) oven for 25 to 30 minutes. Cool completely.

Place cake on a serving platter and chill. Spread crushed strawberries (no juice) or strawberry jam over top of cake. Spread whipped cream over tops and sides. Chill cake thoroughly.

Meanwhile, prepare frosting. Place squares of semisweet chocolate and butter in top of a double boiler. Melt over boiling water, beating well. Cool to lukewarm and spoon over top of chilled cake.

Strawberry-Rhubarb Parfait

I've always been attracted to parfait glasses and hankered to fill them with something . . . simple. Once your pantry shelves are filled with delicious fruit products, infinite combinations are possible. If the tender stalks of rhubarb are no longer available, make stewed rhubarb from the cut-up frozen stalks [p. 45].

Stewed rhubarb
Whipped cream
Chunky strawberry sauce

In the parfait glass, layer stewed rhubarb, whipped cream, and chunky strawberry sauce in that order; repeat until glass is filled. Top with a perfect strawberry. Chill and serve. Don't forget the long-handled spoons.

Raspberries

It's odd, but in an era of relative abundance, many look back with nostalgia to the days before convenience foods, supermarkets, and super highways. Many long for the time when they could buy locally produced, freshly picked raspberries by the quart, as many as they liked, for preserving or for eating fresh with lots of *real,* thick sweet cream, the top cream poured off the pasteurized milk delivered in glass bottles by the local milkman.

In 1858, in just one small area of New York State, 1 million pints of fresh raspberries were shipped to market. By the 1960s, commercial raspberry production had declined drastically. Now fresh raspberries are seldom seen on the market, and when they do appear, they are so expensive that buying enough for a breakfast bowlful seems like the height of extravagance.

The decline in commercial raspberry production coincided with the development of modern agriculture, which is based on mechanization, centralization of production, and mass marketing. Raspberry production thrived when agriculture used primarily hand labor. A good picker could harvest 200 lb (100 kg) fruit a day; five pickers could harvest an acre every two days. The fruit was then quickly shipped to nearby markets, essential for successful raspberry production because the delicate berries deteriorate rapidly in transit. Now the areas of cultivation are so far away from market that the produce is usually sold processed rather than fresh. As for top cream and the milkman, forget it.

Of course, picking wild raspberries is an alternative, but cultivated raspberries are superior in size and flavor. Moreover, cultivated plants are prolific: anyone with enough backyard space to plant 12 canes can expect to harvest 10 to 15 qt (10 to 15 L) a season—*if* the plants are well cared for. This means supplying the plants with plenty of moisture and enriched well-drained soil, and keeping the patch free of weeds; if perennial weeds take hold, the patch is doomed. These conditions, though not difficult, must be met every year to ensure a bountiful harvest. Neglect will result in fewer, smaller berries, weak, diseased plants, and eventually death of the whole planting. If planted and cared for conscientiously, a patch will last almost indefinitely; and by choosing two different varieties, the season can be extended. Berries by the bowlful will be standard breakfast fare—for generous amounts of thick cream, tether a Jersey cow in your yard—and there will be lots left over for preserving.

Planting

The good news is that there are numerous varieties of raspberries to choose from to suit your particular needs and climate, not only traditional red berries, but purple, black, even yellow. The development of fall-bearing types has opened up new possibilities for a late crop of berries, too, but they need to be managed to produce a full late crop in the north (see below). No matter which types you buy, select a sunny spot out of the wind if possible, but not a frost pocket. A slope with a northern exposure is often recommended because it conserves moisture, so important for high-quality production. Also, such a site is not so susceptible to winter freezing and thawing, which causes plants to heave. If a northern exposure is not possible, however, plant canes wherever drainage conditions are good.

Prepare the spot a season ahead by plowing or digging up the earth and enriching it with compost or manure, as recommended for strawberry production. Raspberry canes tolerate a wide range of soils, but, in addition to good drainage, they must be supplied with nutrients. In northern areas, plant canes in the spring rather than the fall so that the roots have time to establish themselves before winter.

To plant, mark rows about 4 ft (1.25 m) apart, using string; two to four 40-ft (12-m) rows are more than adequate for the average family, ensuring a good supply of fresh berries. Along the rows, make holes at 2-ft (60-cm) intervals: push a spade about 6 inches (15 cm) into the soil, and work it back and forth until there is an opening about 2 inches (5 cm) wide. This spacing is a little closer than ordinarily recommended. Close planting will provide just enough shade to help conserve moisture, which encourages the production of larger berries.

Trim each cane to about 6 inches (15 cm). Water each hole and then plant each cane, firmly tamping the dirt around the roots with your feet. In a dry spell, water the plants regularly until they show new growth.

Cultivating

Successful cultivation involves yearly fertilizing, mulching, pruning, and topping. It also entails making and adjusting supports for keeping the canes in neat rows.

In the late fall or winter, following the spring planting, fertilize the raspberries by heaping well-rotted compost or manure on the dormant plants. The next spring, the first season of bearing, put mulch between the rows. Lay down a thick layer of paper and cover it with several inches of *rotted* sawdust or wood chips. This mulch will reduce weeds, conserve moisture and, not least of all, make it easier to walk up and down the rows during harvesting. When the time comes, you will see that this sawdust carpet is a blessing.

Because raspberry plants are biennial, fruiting always occurs in the second year. After fruiting, canes that have produced berries must be pruned from the plants, either by hand or with small clippers. In places where winters are severe, with lots of wind and blowing snow, it is best to wait until early spring to remove old canes because they will help protect young, tender canes from whipping. It is easy to distinguish old canes from new: old ones are tan and brittle, and they break easily. After they are removed, lay them down between the rows as added mulch.

Each spring, renew the paper-sawdust mulch and remove suckers, or secondary shoots, that have grown between the rows. Allow each row to fill out about 12 inches (30 cm), removing overcrowded plants and weak canes. Top off tall canes with hand clippers so that berries can be picked conveniently.

Make supports for the patch. Pound a 6-ft (2-m) wooden or metal post into the ground at the beginning, middle, and end of each row. Attach two 18-inch (45-cm) crosspieces to each post, one about 2 ft (60 cm) from the ground, the other about 4 ft (1.25 m). On the left end of the top crosspiece at the beginning of the row, attach strong cord or wire. String the cord to the center post, wrap it around the left end of the top crosspiece, pulling the cord taut. String the cord to the third post and wrap it securely around the left end of the corresponding crosspiece. Pull the cord around to the right end of that crosspiece and proceed up the other side of the row. Repeat the process for the bottom crosspieces. The raspberry canes will then be tightly penned in.

Tuck all canes inside these supports each spring; ruthlessly remove ones growing outside. Tighten the cords when necessary. Wooden posts will likely need replacing eventually, but if you treat the part below ground with creosote, as fence posts are, they will last at least 10 years, depending on the climate.

Fall-bearing raspberries are vigorous plants. If left on their own, wintered-over canes will produce fruit in summer, but the fall crop will be reduced. To get a full crop of fall berries, cut back canes after frost or at the end of winter, before the new growing season begins. The following season, as new plants grow up, remove the outside suckers and thin plants to about 6 inches (15 cm) apart. The remaining plants will put all their effort into producing a later, more plentiful crop of berries, by September and October in the north.

Harvesting

Harvesting is the culmination of all your work, literally the fruit of your labor. In northern climates, the raspberry season usually begins in mid- to late July, and picking the large moist berries will become a pleasant morning occupation. Use 1-pt (500-mL) containers for picking to prevent the berries on the bottom from being squashed. Unless you plan to eat raspberries for breakfast, wait until the sun has dried the dew: raspberries keep better if they are not damp. (For this reason, use rained-on fruit for cooked dishes, sauces, or juice.) Do not forget to pick the berries closest to the ground, as this well-shaded fruit often grows the largest. And, of course, do not pick raspberries with their stems. It's not easy to do, but I have seen it done.

Preserving, Canning, Freezing, And Cooking

Surely, jam is the most popular raspberry product. Raspberries contain plenty of natural pectin, so when they are mixed with the right amount of sugar, they make a firm jam. Canned raspberries, like canned strawberries, are simple to make. The berries break down somewhat during processing, but the result is still delicious. Berries frozen with a little sugar maintain their shape

better. Red currants will be ripening while raspberries are still plentiful, so do not be afraid to mix the two, in preserves, juices, jams—whatever you like. (Check the chapter on red currants for more ideas.) Raspberry juice and wine is for the end of the harvest, when you have made enough jam and preserves. Raspberries are splendid in baking, too: in cakes, tarts, squares, or puddings.

No matter what you choose to do with your harvest, however, do it without delay! Raspberries deteriorate almost as soon as they are picked. You can refrigerate them for two or three days, but the quality does not compare to that of newly picked fruit. Review Short Course [p. 3–14] before preserving. Use the directions and recipes below for black raspberries. But keep in mind that these are seedier.

Raspberry Jam

The basic approach to jam making, outlined in the recipe The World's Best Strawberry Jam, holds true for raspberry jam as well. Use a mixture of ripe and underripe raspberries.

Makes 1 1/2 to 2 pt (750 mL to 1 L)

1 qt raspberries 1 L
3 scant cups sugar (750 mL)

In a large stainless-steel pot, lightly mash raspberries. Simmer, covered, until bubbling. Stir in sugar and bring to a boil. Stirring as necessary, boil, uncovered, for about 10 minutes or until mixture thickens and begins to cling to bottom of pot.

Remove jam from heat and let subside. Stir, skimming if desired. Fill hot scalded jars [p. 28] to 1/4 inch (5 mm) from the top and seal at once with snap lids and screw bands. Process in a boiling-water bath [p. 26] or steam canner for 15 minutes.

Raspberries Canned in Red Currant Juice

This is the easiest and most delicious way to preserve whole raspberries. Use firm just-ripe raspberries and ripe red currants.

Makes about 6 qt (6 L)

4 qt red currants with stems (4 L)
8 qt raspberries (8 L)
12 cups sugar (3 L)

Prepare red currant juice. In a large preserving pot, combine red currants with a little water. Mash currants, cover, and simmer until currants lose color and juice runs freely. Stir often to prevent sticking. Strain mixture through a jelly bag [p. 28] and let drip for several hours or overnight.

Bring juice to a boil, uncovered, and stir in sugar. Reduce heat and cook mixture slowly for 20 minutes. Gently stir in raspberries and bring mixture to boiling point.

Remove preserves from heat. Ladle into hot scalded jars [p. 28], leaving 1/2 inch (1 cm) headroom, and seal at once with snap lids and screw bands. Process 15 minutes in a boiling-water bath [p. 26] or steam canner.

Plain Canned Raspberry Preserves I

Even if you can't preserve your abundant harvest of raspberries in red currant syrup, you can preserve them in a light sugar-and-water syrup. Use firm ripe raspberries.

Makes 5 to 6 qt (5 to 6 L)

Light syrup:
8 qt raspberries (8 L)
4 cups sugar (1 L)
2 qt water (2 L)

Prepare syrup. In a large stainless-steel pot, combine sugar and water. Stir constantly and bring mixture to a boil.

Place raspberries in a large preserving pot. Add syrup. Keeping pot on simmer, let berries sit in syrup until heated through.

Remove preserves from heat. Ladle into hot scalded canning jars [p. 28], leaving 1/2 inch (1 cm) headroom, and adjust lids. Process jars in a boiling-water bath [p. 26] or steam canner. Process 1-pt (500-mL) jars for 15 minutes, 1-qt (1-L) jars for 20.

Note: To make with honey, reduce sugar to 1 1/2 cups (375 mL) and add 1 1/2 cups (375 ml.) honey.

Plain Canned Raspberry Preserves II

Raspberries preserved this way are not quite so firm as those preserved in syrup, but they are as flavorful. If you have a lot of berries, use several pots for layering the fruit and sugar so the fruit doesn't break down too much when heated. Use firm ripe raspberries.

Makes 3 to 4 qt (3 to 4 L)

6 qt raspberries (6 L)
Sugar

In a large preserving pot, layer raspberries and sugar consecutively until pot is no more than half full. Use 1/2 to 1 cup (125 to 250 mL) sugar to each qt (L) raspberries. Cover and let stand overnight to draw out juices.

Heat mixture slowly, stirring gently with a long-handled wooden spoon to prevent scorching. Bring to boiling point.

Remove preserves from heat. Ladle into hot scalded canning jars [p. 28], leaving 1/2 inch (1 cm) headroom, and adjust lids. Process jars in a boiling-water bath [p. 26] or steam canner for 15 minutes.

Freezing Raspberries

Use 1/2 cup sugar (125 mL) for each quart (1L) of berries. Place berries in a freezer container, add the sugar, gently shaking it in to coat the fruit. To freeze them for making into jam later in the season, spread the berries on a cookie sheet. Place it flat in the freezer. When the berries are frozen, put them in a freezer container without sugar and freeze.

Raspberry Sass

SOME PEOPLE PREFER THIS ON PANCAKES TO ANYTHING ELSE, EVEN MAPLE SYRUP. RASPBERRIES FOR SASS CAN BE A LITTLE LESS FIRM THAN THOSE USED FOR JAM OR FOR CANNED PRESERVES.

Makes about 1 ½ qt (1.5 L)

2 qt raspberries (2 L)
4 cups sugar (1 L)

In a large stainless-steel pot, heat raspberries, covered, until juice begins to run. Stir in sugar and bring to a boil. Reduce heat and simmer, uncovered, for about 10 minutes or until mixture thickens.

Remove sass from heat. Stir. Pour into hot scalded jars [p. 28], leaving 1/2 inch (1 cm) headroom, and seal at once with snap lids and screw bands. Process in a boiling-water bath [p. 26] or steam canner for 15 minutes.

Raspberry-Red Currant Sass

Use quite ripe raspberries for this extravagant sass. You will never taste anything like it.

Makes 2½ to 3 qt (2.5 to 3 L)

1 qt red currants with stems (1 L)
4 qt raspberries (4 L)
2 cups (an approximation, based on the mL amount provided) water (500 mL)
Sugar

Prepare red currant juice. In a large stainless-steel pot, combine red currants and water. Mash currants, cover, and simmer until white, stirring often. Strain through a jelly bag [p. 28] and let drip for several hours or overnight. Measure 2 cups (500 mL) juice.

In a separate pot, crush raspberries. Cover with currant juice and let stand for 10 to 15 minutes. Bring to a boil and simmer for 20 minutes. Stir in sugar, bring mixture to a boil again, and boil, uncovered, for 5 minutes.

Remove sass from heat and let subside. Stir. Pour into hot scalded jars [p. 28], leaving 1/2 inch (1 cm) headroom, and seal at once with snap lids and screw bands. Process in a boiling-water bath [p.28] or steam canner for 10 minutes.

Raspberry Juice

This juice has an incredible color and flavor. When serving raspberry juice, dilute it with water to taste. Use dead-ripe and overripe raspberries.

Makes 2 to 3 qt (2 to 3 L)

6 qt raspberries (6 L)
Sugar
2 cups water (500 mL)

In a large preserving pot, mash raspberries thoroughly. Add water to prevent scorching. Stirring frequently, simmer raspberries, covered, until juice runs freely. Strain mixture through a jelly bag [p. 28] and let drip for several hours or overnight.

Measure juice. Cover and bring to a boil. Stir in 1/2 to 1 cup (125 to 250 mL) sugar to each qt (L) juice. Bring to a boil again, reduce heat, and simmer, uncovered, for 5 minutes.

Remove juice from heat. Pour into hot scalded jars [p. 26], leaving 1/2 inch (1 cm) headroom, and seal at once with snap lids and screw bands. Process in a boiling-water bath [p. 28] or steam canner for 15 minutes.

Variation: To make *raspberry-red currant juice,* substitute red currants with stems for half the raspberries. (Actually, any proportion is fine.) The blending of these two fruits, of the sweet and the tart, results in a distinctive, refreshing flavor that can be found only in your kitchen or in a fancy specialty shop.

Raspberry-Flavored White Wine

A SHORT CUT TO WINE MAKING. PICK RIPE OR OVERRIPE RASPBERRIES—*NOT* RAINED-ON, AS THEY ENCOURAGE MOLD—AND CHOOSE A FAVORITE WINE.

Makes about 3 qt (3 L)

4 to 5 qt raspberries (4 to 5 L)
2 qt white wine (2 L)
2 cups sugar (500 mL)

In a large preserving pot, mash raspberries. Strain through a jelly bag [p. 28]. Measure 1 qt (1 L) juice and place in a container. Add sugar, stir, cover, and let stand for 3 days.

In a separate container, combine juice and white wine. Bottle and seal at once. Let stand at least a week before tasting.

Raspberry-Jam Squares

THE FRESH FLAVOR OF THE JAM GIVES THESE SQUARES THEIR DISTINCTION.

Makes 15 squares

2 cups flour (500 mL)
1 /4 cup ice water (50 mL)
1/2 tsp salt (2 mL)
1 pt raspberry jam [p. 67] (500 mL)
2/3 cup shortening or lard (150 mL)
1 egg yolk

Sift together flour and salt. With a pastry blender, cut in half the shortening until mixture forms peas. Cut in remaining shortening. Gradually sprinkle cold water on dough, mixing at same time. Handle dough as little as possible.

Grease an 8-inch x 12-inch (3-L) baking pan. Press half the dough onto bottom of pan. Cover evenly with jam.

Roll out remaining dough on a board, adding flour if necessary to make a pliable dough, and place on top of jam. Lightly beat egg yolk and brush over top crust. Prick crust a few times with a fork. Bake in a 350°F (180°C) oven for 35 minutes or until crust is lightly browned. Cool and cut into squares.

Note: If you do not have raspberry jam, many other kinds will make good substitutes. Red currant jam [p. 81] or gooseberry jam [p. 93] are particularly good, as is Gooseberry-Red Currant Bar-le-Duc [p. 92].

Raspberry Pudding, or Rothe Gruetze

THIS IS A EUROPEAN VARIATION OF MENNONITE *MOOS*, OR FRUIT SOUP.

Serves 6

4 cups ripe raspberries (1 L)
1/3 cup cornstarch (75 mL)
4 cups ripe red currants (1 L)
1 1/2 cups sugar (375 mL)
4 cups cold water (1 L)
Whipped cream [p. 58]

In a large pot, combine raspberries, red currants, and cold water. Bring to a boil and boil until fruit is tender, about 5 minutes. Mash berries and strain, reserving juice. In a cup, dissolve cornstarch in a little water.

Add sugar to reserved juice. Bring mixture to a boil and add cornstarch. Stirring constantly, simmer until thick. Pour into custard cups and chill. Serve with whipped cream.

Raspberry Spritz

RESERVE THIS RECIPE FOR CHRISTMAS, NEW YEAR'S, OR A SPECIAL OCCASION.

Makes 15 squares

2 cups butter, softened (500 mL)
2 tsp vanilla (10 mL)
1 cup sugar (250 mL)
4 cups flour (1 L)
1 egg
Raspberry jam [p. 67]
1 tsp salt (5 mL)

In a large bowl, cream together butter and sugar. Beat in egg, salt, and vanilla. Gradually add flour, mixing until dough is formed.

Press slightly more than half the dough onto an ungreased cookie sheet, spreading to 1/4 inch (5 mm) thick. Generously cover with jam.

Roll out remaining dough on a board. Using a star-shaped cookie cutter, cut shapes. Place stars on top of jam, about 3 to a row. Bake in a 400°F (200°C) oven for 15 minutes or until stars are golden brown. Cool and cut into star-shaped squares.

Raspberry Pudding

Raspberry Slump

Slump, like *grunt,* is a New England term for a pudding-like dessert. It is difficult to sort out all these puddings and define their differences. Nonetheless, grunts are usually steamed for several hours; slumps are often cooked on top of the stove. This slump, however, is neither steamed nor cooked. It is baked. Serve it hot with thick sweet cream or thinned Devonshire cream [p. 57].

Serves 4

1 qt ripe raspberries (1 L)
1 1/2 tsp baking powder (7 mL)
Handful ripe red currants
1/2 tsp salt (2 mL)
1 3/4 cups sugar (425 mL)
2 Tbsp melted butter (25 mL)
1 cup flour (250 mL)
1/2 cup milk (125 mL)

Place raspberries and red currants in a buttered baking dish and sprinkle with 1/4 cup (50 mL) sugar.

In a large bowl, mix together 1 1/2 cups (375 mL) sugar, flour, baking powder, salt, melted butter, and milk until a batter is formed.

Pour batter over raspberries and smooth out to cover. Bake in a 350°F (180°C) oven for 35 minutes or until juice starts to bubble over crust.

Chocolate Cake Supreme

3/4 cup butter (175 mL)
1 tsp baking powder (5 mL)
2 eggs
Dash salt
1 tsp vanilla (65 mL)
1/3 cup cocoa (75 mL)
2 cups flour (500 mL)
1 cup cold water (250 mL)
1 1/2 cups sugar (375 mL)
Raspberry jam [p. 67]
1 tsp baking soda (5 mL)
Whipped cream [p. 58]
Ripe raspberries

In a large bowl, cream butter. Beat in eggs one at a time and add vanilla. Sift together flour, sugar, baking soda, baking powder, salt, and cocoa. Add sifted ingredients and cold water alternately to butter-egg mixture. Beat after each addition.

Pour batter into a greased 9-inch (3-L) angel-food cake pan. Bake in a 350°F (180°C) oven for about 30 minutes or until a knife or cake tester inserted near center comes out clean.

Cool cake. Cut into 3 layers and spread a thick coating of jam between each and on top of cake. Garnish each piece with whipped cream and ripe raspberries.

Super Chocolate Roll

5 eggs, separated
1 to 2 tsp vanilla (5 to 10 mL)
1 cup sifted icing sugar (250 mL)
Raspberry jam [p. 67]
3 Tbsp cocoa (50 mL)
Whipped cream [p. 58]

Line a shallow 10-inch x 14-inch (2-L) cake pan with foil, and grease foil with butter.

In a large bowl, beat egg whites into soft peaks. Add icing sugar 1 Tbsp (15 mL) at a time, beating constantly. Using a whisk, beat in cocoa.

In a separate bowl, beat egg yolks. With a rubber spatula, fold yolks into egg-cocoa mixture. Add vanilla to taste. Pour batter into prepared pan, spreading evenly. Bake in a 350°F (180°C) oven for about 20 minutes. Remove from oven and spread a damp dish towel over cake.

Sprinkle a dry dish towel with icing sugar. When cake has cooled slightly, remove damp cloth and turn cake onto icing-sugar towel. Carefully loosen corners of foil and tear it off. Roll up cake in icing-sugar towel and cool completely.

Unroll cake and cover top with a thick layer of jam. Without towel, roll up cake again, jam side in. Cover jellyroll completely with whipped cream. Chill for about 2 hours before serving

Red Currants

Like raspberries, red currants did not survive the transition from "old-fashioned" farming to high-technology "agribiz." These juicy berries deteriorate rapidly in transit, they are harder to pick than other small fruits, and they grow best in cold climates, so they are not so adaptable as, say, strawberries. Altogether, they do not suit modern agriculture or mass marketing.

It is hard to believe that red currants were so highly prized in the early 20th century. Nearly every garden had at least a red currant bush or two, and local markets sold thousands of bushels of currants each year. No decent housekeeper neglected to store enough berries for the annual jelly making. What well-stocked cupboard did not include jars of the clear red jelly, rich in pectin and vitamin C, esteemed as much for gracing a roast as for soothing a fever or a burn? You can look for a jar of this heretofore treasured jelly on the supermarket shelf, but you look in vain.

Fashions are cyclical, however, and once more red currants are being looked on with favor by the home gardener. If they do not suit modern agricultural techniques, they are more than suitable for the backyard fruit garden. Red currant shrubs are attractive in any season, they bear well, and their produce can be turned into a number of sought-after products. Gardeners need have only a few shrubs, for they alone will provide enough berries to make the legendary jelly, as well as other old-time favorites.

One word of caution. Red currants, along with black currants and gooseberries, belong to the genus *Ribes* and therefore may carry the fungus white-pine blister rust. If there are white pines on your property or in your area, plant currants 1000 ft (300 m) away from stands of the trees. Check with the local Cooperative Extension office to find out if there are any restrictions against *Ribes* in your area (see Appendix; also for mail order sources for this specialty fruit).

Planting

Buy two or three plants—perhaps two varieties, an early-and later-ripening one. Red Lake, for example, is a commonly grown variety, and two bushes will produce 6 to 12 qt (6 to 12 L) currants. Like many small fruits, red currants do best if the shrubs are planted on a slope with a northern exposure, providing just the right amount of sun and shade and drainage for bountiful fruiting. They thrive particularly well in rich clay loam.

Plant in early spring, when bushes are dormant. Trim plants to 4 to 6 inches (10 to 15 cm) in height and put them in a bucket of water while preparing holes. With a spade, make holes about 5 ft (1.5 m) apart and deep enough to accommodate the roots of the plants. If you have several plants, dig the holes in rows about 6 to 10 ft (2 to 3 m) apart. Do not be surprised by the gaps in this spacing. The small rootstocks will, in a few years' time, spread out into handsome bushes that will fill in the empty areas.

Add a shovelful of well-rotted compost to each hole, water the holes, and set in the plants, carefully placing the roots over a small mound of soil and firmly tamping down the earth around them. If there is a dry spell following planting, water the plants regularly until they show signs of new growth.

Cultivating

Spread a 2-ft (60-cm) wide ring of well-rotted compost or manure around each plant the following spring, the first season of growth, when the ground has warmed up. On top of the compost, put down a layer of thick paper, heavy cardboard, old cloth grain bags, or worn-out nonsynthetic carpet and then a layer of old hay, straw, or if you live near the shore, eel grass if available, to hold down the paper. All these layers will eventually break down and form a nutritious mulch that will help conserve moisture and prevent weeds and grass from competing with the currants for nutrients. Renew these layers once a year, in spring or fall.

As the currant bushes grow, the bottom stems will spread out close to the ground. Therefore, keep the grass well mown all around the shrubs so that the fruit on the lower branches does not become entangled in grass.

In the early spring, prune out dead wood, as well as stems that look old. Until they are three years old, literature on the subject says red currant bushes should have no more than 10 to 12 stems. Vigorous bushes, however, can support more. It is hard to tell the age of each stem, but, in general, young stems are gray, and older ones are brown. The oldest stems are dark brown and knobby and have a smooth bark. Prune out the oldest stems and less vigorous older ones. Trim the lower branches of mature bushes as well if you wish to encourage an upright habit of growth.

You may prefer the sprawling habit, however. Such bushes are graceful as they sweep to the ground, and their bottom branches may "layer" themselves, or set down roots. In the spring, increase your supply of plants. Sever the rooted stem from the parent plant, and replant it in a prepared nursery bed that is protected from the wind and that has well-drained, fertile, friable soil. Set these plants fairly close together in rows and plant them rather deep. Water them well and transfer them to a permanent site the following spring.

In June, when the stems begin to form flower buds, watch out for the currant sawfly, whose larvae look like small green inchworms about three quarters of an inch long. These insects, if undeterred, can strip a plant of its leaves in no time. If they are evident, spray the bushes with a pyrethrin-based insecticide. We like Pyola (see Appendix for a source), an effective, organic spray that attacks insect adults, larvae, and eggs. Consult your local Cooperative Extension office for other sprays or dusts. Whatever you use, repeat the treatment a week later and until there is no more damage to the bush.

Harvesting

Red currants grow in clusters, turning from green to pale red to bright red. Not surprisingly, the fruit at the top of the bush usually ripens first; the berries at the bottom, last. In the northeast, red currants can be harvested in midsummer. For jelly, pick a mixture of ripe (top) and underripe (bottom) berries; for jam, a majority of ripe; for sauce, all ripe; for juice and wine, dead ripe or overripe. To pick fruit for jelly, juice, or wine, run your fingers down the main stems of the clusters, leaving the little stem on each berry intact. For jam and sass, pick each berry off its stem.

Preserving, Freezing, And Cooking

If you are going to grow red currants, you are obliged to make red currant jelly. In the following pages, there are two recipes to choose from. Throw some raspberries into the jelly bag, and then make Bar-le-Duc. After you have lined your pantry with jars of jelly, move on to red currant jam, sass, juice, and snub. But do not try drying red currants: they are too seedy. Red currants give a refreshingly tart quality to baked goods. Include them in any of the cooking recipes in the preceding chapter or try red currant pie topped with meringue. Review A Short Course in Fruit Preserving [p. 3–14] before preserving. Use white currants the same way as red currants. The variety Pink Champagne, a cross between red and white, is sweeter than either and can be eaten fresh.

Red Currant Jelly I

HERE IS ONE VERSION OF THE FABLED JELLY. EVEN IF YOU DO NOT USE IT TO SOOTHE A FEVERISH BROW OR A BURN, USE IT AS AN ACCOMPANIMENT TO MEAT DISHES. IT IS ALSO GREAT WITH CREAM CHEESE, ON HOT MUFFINS, BISCUITS, OR CORNBREAD. USE A MIXTURE OF RIPE AND UNDERRIPE BERRIES.

Makes 1 1/2 to 2 pt (750 mL to 1 L)

2 1/2 qt red currants with stems (2.5 L)
1 cup water (250 mL)
Sugar

In a large preserving pot, combine red currants and water. Boil, covered, until currants are white, stirring occasionally to prevent sticking. Strain mixture through a jelly bag [p. 28] and let drip for several hours or overnight.

Measure juice and cook 4 cups (1 L) at a time in a large stainless-steel pot. Cover and bring to a boil. Stir in 3/4 cup (175 mL) sugar to each cup (250 mL) juice. Bring to a boil again. Skimming as necessary, boil, uncovered, for about 15 minutes or less or until a small amount sheets off a metal spoon [p. 28-29].

Remove jelly from heat and let subside. Stir, skimming if desired. Fill hot scalded jars [p. 28] to 1/4 inch (5 mm) from the top and seal at once with snap lids and screw bands. Process in a boiling-water bath [p. 26] or steam canner for 10 minutes.

Red Currant Jelly II

THIS JELLY IS LESS INTENSELY FLAVORED THAN RED CURRANT JELLY I. USE A MIXTURE OF RIPE AND UNDERRIPE BERRIES.

Makes about 4 pt (2 L)

4 qt currants with stems (4 L)
1 qt water (1 L)
Sugar

In a large preserving pot, combine red currants and water. Simmer currants, covered, until white, stirring and mashing occasionally. Strain mixture through a jelly bag [p. 28] and let drip for several hours or overnight.

Measure juice and cook 4 cups (1 L) at a time in a large stainless-steel pot. Cover and bring to a boil. Stir in 1 cup (250 mL) sugar to each cup (250 mL) juice. Bring to a boil again. Skimming as necessary, boil, uncovered, until a small amount sheets off a metal spoon [p. 28-29].

Remove jelly from heat and let subside. Stir, skimming if desired. Fill hot scalded jars [p. 28] to 1/4 inch (5 mm) from the top and seal at once with snap lids and screw bands. Process in a boiling-water bath [p. 26] or steam canner for 10 minutes.

Variation: To make *red currant-raspberry jelly*, substitute ripe and underripe raspberries for half the red currants. The proportion isn't crucial, however, so experiment as you please.

Bar-le-Duc Jelly

This is neither a true jelly nor the authentic Bar-le-Duc, named after a city in France. There the seeds of each berry are removed before being made into a concoction that is a cross between a jam and a jelly. The following is what *I* call Bar-le-Duc. Like the real thing, the whole currant is suspended in the jelled juice. For this recipe, use mainly ripe red currants, with some underripe.

Makes 1 1/2 to 2 pt (750 mL to 1 L)

1 qt red currants without stems (1 L)
1/3 cup water (75 mL)
2 cups sugar (500 mL)

In a large stainless-steel pot, combine red currants and water. Cover and simmer until berries are just tender but still whole. Stir in sugar. Stirring gently, cook at a rolling boil, uncovered, until a small amount of mixture sheets off a metal spoon [p. 28-29].

Remove jelly from heat and let subside. Stir, skimming if desired. Fill hot scalded jars [p. 28] to 1/4 inch (5 mm) from the top and seal at once with snap lids and screw bands. Process in a boiling-water bath [p. 26] or steam canner for 10 minutes.

Red Currant Jam

Use mainly ripe red currants, with some underripe.

Makes 1 ½ to 2 pt (750 mL to 1 L)

4 cups red currants without stems (1 L)
2 2/3 cups sugar (650 mL)

In a large stainless-steel pot, mash red currants, cover, and heat until simmering. Stir in sugar and bring to a rolling boil. Stirring occasionally, boil, uncovered, for about 15 minutes or less or until mixture thickens and starts to cling to bottom of pot.

Remove jam from heat and let subside. Stir, skimming if desired. Fill hot scalded jars [p. 28] to 1/4 inch (5 mm) from the top and seal at once with snap lids and screw bands and seal. Process in a boiling-water bath [p. 26] or steam canner for 15 minutes.

Red Currant Sass

POUR A LITTLE RED CURRANT SASS ON BUTTERED PANCAKES, THEN A SPOONFUL OF BRANDIED FRUIT, THEN A DAB OF SOUR CREAM. USE RIPE RED CURRANTS.

Makes about 1 ½ qt (1.5 L)

2 qt red currants without stems (2 L)
3 cups sugar (750 mL)

Layer red currants and sugar consecutively in a large stainless-steel pot. Cover and let stand overnight. Bring mixture to a boil, uncover, and boil for 10 to 15 minutes or until mixture thickens.

Remove sass from heat and let subside. Stir. Pour into hot scalded jars [p. 28], leaving 1/2 inch (1 cm) headroom, and seal at once with snap lids and screw bands. Process in a boiling-water bath [p. 26] or steam canner for 15 minutes.

Red Currant Juice

Makes 2 to 3 qt (2 to 3 L)

6 qt red currants with stems (6 L)
2 cups water (500 mL)
Sugar

In a large preserving pot, mash dead-ripe red currants thoroughly. Add water to prevent scorching. Stirring frequently, simmer, covered, until juice runs freely. Strain mixture through a jelly bag [p. 28] and let drip for several hours or overnight.

Measure juice. Cover and bring to a boil. Stir in 1/2 to 1 cup (125 to 250 mL) sugar to each qt (L) juice. Bring to a boil, reduce heat, and simmer, uncovered, for 5 minutes. Remove juice from heat. Pour into hot scalded jars [p. 28], leaving 1/2 inch (1 cm) headroom, and seal at once with snap lids and screw bands. Process in a boiling-water bath [p. 26] or steam canner for 15 minutes.

Freezing Red Currants

You can easily freeze red currants if you're too busy to turn them into preserves during harvest season. Just pour cleaned, de-stemmed fruit into a freezer container or bag and seal. Or freeze with stems to use later for jelly and juice.

Red Currant Snub

THIS IS A VARIATION OF THE SHRUB DRINK OF NEW ENGLAND. IF YOU LIKE, USE A MIXTURE OF RASPBERRY AND RED CURRANT JUICE. WHEN SERVING SNUB, DILUTE IT WITH WATER TO TASTE AND POUR OVER ICE. OR LEAVE UNDILUTED, SPOON A LITTLE OVER PANCAKES AND TOP THAT WITH SOUR CREAM.

Makes 1 1/2 Pt (750 mL)

1 qt red currants with stems (1 L)
1 teacupful good brandy (175 mL)
2 cups sugar (500 mL)

In a preserving pot, mash red currants and simmer, covered, until white. Strain through a jelly bag [p. 28] and let drip for several hours or overnight.

Measure 1 pt (500 mL) juice. Stir in sugar and boil mixture for 15 minutes. Remove from heat and let cool. Stir in brandy. Bottle and cork immediately. Store lying down in a cool cupboard.

Thumbprint Cookies

THE FIRST TIME I MADE THESE COOKIES IT WAS AT THE END OF THE FRUIT SEASON. I HAPPENED TO HAVE A LOT OF LITTLE JARS OF VARIOUS JAMS AND JELLIES IN THE REFRIGERATOR, SO I TRIED EACH AS A FILLING FOR MY THUMBPRINTS. THE CONSENSUS WAS THAT RED CURRANT JELLY WAS THE BEST, FOLLOWED BY RASPBERRY JAM AND ELDERBERRY JELLY. SEE WHAT YOU THINK.

Makes 2 1/2 dozen

1 full cup butter (250 mL)
2 tsp vanilla (10 mL)
1/2 cup sugar (125 mL)
2 scant cups flour (500 mL)
2 egg yolks
Red currant jelly [p. 79]

In a large bowl, cream butter; beat in sugar. Add egg yolks and beat all. Beat in vanilla and flour. Roll dough into balls the size of walnuts.

Place balls fairly close together on a lightly greased cookie sheet. Press a thumbprint into center of each and fill with red currant jelly (or your favorite jam or jelly). Bake in a 375°F (190°C) oven for 8 to 10 minutes. Note: You can flute sides of unbaked cookies by lightly pressing a sharp fork, held upright, against the edges of the dough, or roll out dough and cut with a fluted cookie cutter.

Thumbprint Cookies

Red Currant Meat Sauce

Makes 1 cup (250 mL)

1 cup red currant jelly [p. 79] (250 mL)
1 1/2 Tbsp chopped mint leaves (20 mL)
Grated orange rind

In a bowl, gently break up jelly with a fork and stir in mint leaves and grated orange rind to taste. Let stand for at least 1 hour before using. Serve with lamb or veal.

Red Currant-Raspberry Tart

USE DEAD-RIPE, NOT OVERRIPE, BERRIES FOR THIS DELICIOUS TART.

3 cups red currants (750 ml)
1 cup raspberries (250 mL)
1 to 2 Tbsp cornstarch (15 to 25 mL)
Sugar to taste
Pastry [p. 46]

In a pot, cook together red currants and raspberries, covered, until soft and juicy. Remove from heat, stir in sugar to taste, and stir in cornstarch. Let stand for 10 minutes.

Pour filling into an unbaked 7-inch (18-cm) pie shell and make a lattice top with strips of dough. Bake in a 375°F (190°C) oven for 30 minutes or until pastry is browned and berries are bubbling.

Red Currant Pie

THIS SELDOM MADE OLD-FASHIONED PIE HAS GREAT FLAVOR AND A MELTING SMOOTHNESS WITH THE DELICATE MERINGUE TOPPING.

1 cup sugar (250 mL)
Unbaked pie shell [p. 46]
1/4 cup pastry flour (50 mL)
2 egg yolks

Meringue:

2 Tbsp water (25 mL)
2 egg whites
1 1/2 cups red currants (375 mL)
4 Tbsp sugar (75 mL)

In a large bowl, combine 1 cup (250 mL) sugar, flour, egg yolks, water, and red currants. Mix well. Pour into an unbaked 7-inch (18-cm) pie shell. Bake in a 350°F (180°C) oven for 35 to 40 minutes or until crust is browned and berries are bubbling.

Prepare meringue. Beat egg whites until stiff, gently folding in 4 Tbsp (75 mL) sugar. Pour meringue on top of baked pie and return to oven for 10 minutes or until meringue is lightly browned.

Gooseberries

North Americans have never been wild about gooseberries. True, gooseberries have been grown for hundreds of years in rural gardens, and there have been times, such as in the 18th century, when they have been prized for medicinal purposes, as well as for making jams, jellies, and pies. But many years have passed since fresh gooseberries have been available in the marketplace. Have you ever seen gooseberries on a grocery-store shelf? In an expensive specialty shop, perhaps. It is probably safe to say that few people under 40 have ever tasted gooseberries in any form.

On the other hand, the mere mention of the word *gooseberry* sends transplanted Europeans into ecstasy. They begin to reminisce about their homeland—gooseberries, it seems, embody the lost charms of a half-remembered rural life. However small their gardens, many expatriate Europeans try to find room to plant at least one gooseberry bush, which in three years bears a fine crop of pale-green or red-striped fruit.

Gooseberries have much to recommend them: their bushes require only a small area to produce an abundant crop (5 to 10 qt/5 to 10 L per bush); their culinary uses are varied (though not so varied as strawberries or raspberries); and their high pectin content guarantees success even for the inexperienced jam or jelly maker. There are things to be said for the bush itself: whether in leaf, bud, bloom, or berry, it is attractive, suitable for planting around a house foundation or even in a corner of a cottage garden flower bed. Depending on the climate, a healthy bush will produce abundantly for 20 years and will stay ornamental for even longer than that. Finally, the shrubs are easy to grow in places where winters are freezing and summers are moderate.

Remember, however, gooseberries, which belong to the genus *Ribes,* are alternate hosts to the disease white-pine blister rust. Check with the local Cooperative Extension office to see if there are any restrictions in your area (see Appendix to locate your local office). Plant gooseberries 1000 ft (300 m) away from any white-pine stands.

Planting

Although gooseberries are making a comeback among home gardeners, with few exceptions, there are still only a few varieties commonly available. In Canada, gooseberry plants may be fairly easy to come by, but in the United States, they are harder to find (see Appendix).

Gooseberry varieties, American or European, vary in color (from green to red), in size, and in time of ripening; in addition, some varieties have fewer thorns and therefore are easier to pick. Here, though, I must say something about what I regard as a cherished myth: red gooseberries. Invariably, whenever we have ordered a so-called red variety, it has turned out to be green. Not that we really mind, but I do wish plant nurseries would stop saying that every variety they offer is red; even the ubiquitous Pixwell, which everyone knows is green, is described in one catalog as pink. Poorman is offered as "brilliant" red; Clark (a European type), red; and Captivator, "dull" red and "almost" thornless. In any event, it probably won't matter, as Pixwell is, with few exceptions, the only one available. Recently, however, I saw a picture in a plant nursery catalogue where the gooseberries really *did* look red. Maybe they really are.

Once you have tracked some down, choose a slope with a northern exposure for planting if possible. Gooseberries thrive where it is cool, though *not* shady. The roots appreciate the good drainage and protection of a slope: they need to be shielded from excessive sun, which could scald them, and excessive shade, which could cause mildew. Soil that is a little too wet for other fruits suits gooseberries just fine as long as the roots are not standing in water (fertile clay loam is preferable). Few plants survive wet feet.

It is best to plant gooseberry shrubs in the spring, when they are dormant. To plant, trim rootstocks to 4 to 6 inches (10 to 15 cm) and put each one in a bucket of water while preparing holes. With a spade, make the holes 5 ft (1.5 m) apart and as deep as necessary to accommodate the roots. If you are planting several bushes, make rows about 6 to 10 ft (2 to 3 m) apart. Add a shovelful of well-rotted compost to each hole, water the holes, and plant the rootstocks in a little mound of earth, firmly tamping down the soil around them. In a dry spell, water the plants regularly until they show signs of new growth.

Cultivating

After planting, mulching is in order. This helps eliminate weeds, creates cool, moist conditions, and builds up the soil. In a 2-ft (60-cm) wide ring around each plant, set down a layer of

well-rotted compost or manure, a layer of heavy paper, cardboard, or worn-out nonsynthetic carpet, and a layer of hay, straw, or, as we used in Cape Breton, eel grass. Renew this mulch each spring or fall.

Do not do much pruning the first few years after planting. In the early spring, remove dead or damaged branches with hand clippers. After the third year, when the gooseberry bushes get into high production, do a little more pruning if necessary but not much. The older the plant gets, though, the more you should prune every spring. Pay particular attention to the center of the plant, which should be kept airy because crowded branches encourage disease, powdery mildew in particular. A wet summer, together with a bush with too many stems, spells trouble. After removing the dead and damaged branches, remove any that are more than three years old so that the bush is left with a combination of one-, two-, and three-year-old branches. Fruit is produced on one-year-old wood and on the spurs of older wood. Also, many books recommend leaving only 5 to 7 shoots per plant, but more than a dozen can be left on vigorous bushes if they are not overcrowded.

Prune branches lying close to the ground if you wish to encourage an upright habit of growth—and if you do not like searching for berries tangled in grass. I prefer the sprawling habit because I like to find hidden treasures. There is always the possibility, too, that the low-lying branches will "layer" themselves, that is, send out roots into the ground.

Unfortunately, the hardier American gooseberry varieties do not layer themselves so readily as the European types, but a diligent search in the spring among low branches should yield a few plants. Roots can grow from more than one place on a single branch, so with judicious cutting, you can make several little plants. Set them fairly close together in weed-free, loose, and well-drained soil, and water and continue to weed thoroughly. Let the plants grow a year before transferring them to a permanent site. If the summer is wet, extra watering, of course, is not necessary.

There are two other, more difficult ways to propagate gooseberries. The first method is to make cuttings from new wood in the early spring. Choose medium-sized shoots that are 8 to 10 inches (20 to 25 cm) long and plant them 6 inches (15 cm) apart in cultivated garden soil. The secret to success with these cuttings is *deep* planting: leave only 1 to 2 buds above ground. Alternatively, plant these cuttings in pots or beds in a cold frame or greenhouse as long as the soil is well worked and friable. Wherever you plant them, water them well during the growing season, protect them with straw in the late fall, and make sure they are not exposed to freezing temperatures. Following these rules, you should have healthy new plants the next spring.

The other method is "mound" layering. In August, after harvest, cut back the main branches severely to encourage new growth from the bottom of the plant. When new shoots begin to grow, heap dirt around them to encourage rooting. By autumn, or by the following spring, the new shoots should be well rooted. Detach them with clippers, plant them fairly deep in a well-prepared bed, and water and weed them. The next spring, move them to their permanent location. Once new plants are in their permanent site, mulch and prune as for other bushes.

One essential task for all bushes, new and old, is to watch out for an invasion of currant sawflies, little green worms, early in the growing season, before berries are formed. These insects, about three quarters of an inch long, can strip a plant entirely of its leaves overnight. If you see any sign of them, spray your bushes on a still day with a pyrethrin-based insecticide; we like the organic spray, Pyola, which works. Whatever you use, repeat the treatment a week later. Consult your local Cooperative Extension office for recommendations (see Appendix).

Harvesting

Like all fruits, gooseberries have three stages of ripening: underripe, ripe, and overripe. It is difficult for the novice to figure out exactly when to pick the fruit, so it is a good idea to keep the following pointers in mind. Underripe gooseberries are green in color, quite hard, and should be picked for jelly making. There is no need to rush out and pick these berries immediately, however, for they stand on the bush well, for a week, anyway. When gooseberries reach the ripe stage, they are still firm but not quite so hard, and their color has not changed noticeably. These berries are best for jams, canning, preserves, pies, and tarts, as well as for eating chilled, especially on a hot day. It is not advisable to wait for the third stage. By that time, many berries will have fallen to the ground and will have been quickly harvested by eager birds. Sometimes one is advised to wait until the fruit has turned yellowish (if it's a green variety) or dark red (if a red type) before harvesting, but experience proves that this is not practical. The fruit is supposed to be

sweetest at this stage, but only the birds know for sure.

Preserving, Canning, Freezing, And Cooking

Someday I hope to be remembered with great affection and gratitude by new (and old) generations of gooseberry aficionados for having successfully made dozens of jams, jellies, and what not without removing either the stems (unless very evident) or the tails. No matter what you may read to the contrary, it is not necessary to top and tail gooseberries, an arduous task. I have processed gooseberries both ways, with absolutely no difference in the results, although in jam the tails are visible as dark specks.

Of course, try your hand at the old, reliable jams and jellies. But if you have an abundance of fruit, try chutney, marmalade (my favorite), and preserves. Gooseberries are also prized for pies and tarts; for these, use firm ripe berries. Though not so versatile as some other small fruits, gooseberries have special qualities that are irreplaceable. When underripe, they are delightfully sour; when ripe, they resemble green grapes—sweet with a little zing. Review Short Course [p. 3-14] before preserving.

Gooseberry Jelly

ALTHOUGH MOST GOOSEBERRIES ARE GREEN, THEIR JELLY IS A LOVELY SHADE OF AMBER-RED. THIS JELLY HAS A DISTINCT, DELICATE FLAVOR, AND IT IS ATTRACTIVE—PERFECT FOR GIFT GIVING. USE UNDERRIPE BERRIES.

Makes about 3 pt (1.5 L)

3 lb gooseberries (1.5 kg)
Sugar
4 1/2 cups cold water (1.125 L)

In a large preserving pot, cover gooseberries with water. Simmer, covered, until soft, mashing when berries begin to cook. Be careful not to scorch fruit. Strain mixture through a jelly bag [p. 28] and let drip for several hours or overnight.

Measure juice and cook 4 cups (1 L) at a time in a large stainless-steel pot. Cover and bring to a boil. Stir in 1 cup (250 mL) sugar to each cup (250 mL) juice. Skimming as necessary, cook at a rolling boil, uncovered, for 10 to 15 minutes or until a small amount sheets off a metal spoon [p. 28-29].

Remove jelly from heat and let subside. Stir, skimming if desired. Fill hot scalded jars [p. 28] to 1/4 inch (5 mm) from the top and seal at once with snap lids and screw bands. Process in a boiling-water bath [p. 26] or steam canner for 10 minutes.

Note: 3 lb (1.5 kg) gooseberries equals about 6 heaping cups (1. 5 L).

Gooseberry-Elderflower Jelly

Making this jelly is one of the anticipated joys of summer. When the bank of elderberry plants is in blossom, we quickly harvest some gooseberries, the ones we have been saving just for this treat. It is the tension between anticipating the elderflowers and watching over the gooseberries that gives this jelly a special place. Besides, it is delicious—the elderflowers add a grapelike flavor. Use slightly underripe gooseberries.

Makes 4 to 6 Pt (1 to 1.5 L)

6 lb gooseberries (3 kg)
3 to 4 large bunches elder-flowers with short stems
1 1/2 pt water (750 mL)
Sugar

In a large preserving pot, cover gooseberries with water. Simmer, covered, until soft, stirring occasionally and mashing to form a pulp. Strain through a jelly bag [p. 28] and let drip for several hours or overnight.

Tie up elderflowers in a cheesecloth or muslin bag. Measure juice and cook 4 cups (1 L) at a time in a large stainless-steel pot. Cover, bring to a boil, and stir in 1 cup (250 mL) sugar to each cup (250 mL) juice. Bring to a boil again and add elderflowers. Skimming as necessary, boil, uncovered, until a small amount sheets off a metal spoon [p. 28-29].

Remove jelly from heat and retrieve elderflowers. Let subside and stir, skimming if desired. Fill hot scalded jars [p. 28] to 1/4 inch (5 mm) from the top and seal at once with snap lids and screw bands. Process in a boiling-water bath [p. 26] or steam canner for 10 minutes.

Gooseberry-Red Currant Bar-le-Duc

This is an intriguing variation of Bar-le-Duc jelly. Use slightly ripe gooseberries and ripe, not too soft, red currants. When cooking, try to leave the berries whole.

Makes 1 1/2 to 2 pt (750 mL to 1 L)

1 qt gooseberries (1 L)
1/3 cup water (75 mL)
1/2 qt red currants without stems (500 mL)
3 cups sugar (750 mL)

In a large stainless-steel pot, combine gooseberries, red currants, and. water. Stirring gently, heat mixture, covered, until bubbling. Stir in sugar and boil, uncovered, for 10 to 15 minutes or until a small amount sheets off a metal spoon [p. 28-29].

Remove jelly from heat and let subside. Stir, skimming if desired. Fill hot scalded jars [p. 28] to 1/4 inch (5 mm) from the top and seal at once with snap lids and screw bands.

Process in a boiling-water bath [p. 26] or steam canner for 15 minutes.

Gooseberry Jam

When your gooseberries start to soften, the second stage of ripening, make jam. This jam sets quickly, so watch carefully.

Makes 1 1/2 pt (750 mL)

3 cups gooseberries (750 mL)
Water or red currant juice
2 cups sugar (500 mL)
Pinch salt

In a large stainless-steel pot, simmer gooseberries, covered, in a little water or red currant juice to prevent scorching. Mash if desired. When berries are bubbling, stir in sugar and salt. Bring to a boil. Stirring occasionally, boil, uncovered, for 10 to 15 minutes or until mixture thickens and begins to cling to bottom of pot.

Remove jam from heat and let subside. Stir, skimming if desired. Fill hot scalded jars [p. 28] to 1/4 inch (5 mm) from the top and seal at once with snap lids and screw bands. Process in a boiling water bath [p. 26] or steam canner for 15 minutes.

Variation: To make *gooseberry-black currant jam,* substitute 1/2 to 1 cup (125 to 250 mL) black currants for 1/2 to 1 cup (125 to 250 mL) gooseberries. We discovered this jam one summer when we were too busy making hay to pick the gooseberries, most of which fell to the ground. So we mixed black currants with the remaining gooseberries and discovered one of our favorite jams. The new fruit Josta apparently gives the same flavor, and if it does, it is a real bonus for the small-fruit gardener.

Three-Fruit Jam

For every fruit, use a mixture of ripe and slightly underripe berries.

Makes about 5 pt (2.5 L)

1 qt gooseberries (1 L)
1 qt raspberries (1 L)
1 qt red currants (1 L)
Sugar

Weigh fruit. In a large stainless-steel pot, simmer fruit, covered, for 20 minutes, mashing if desired and stirring occasionally to prevent scorching. Stir in a scant 2 cups (500 mL) sugar to each lb (500 g) fruit. Stirring as necessary, cook, uncovered, at a rolling boil for about 10 minutes or until mixture thickens and begins to cling to bottom of pot.

Remove jam from heat and let subside. Stir, skimming if desired. Fill hot scalded jars [p. 28] to 1/4 inch (5 mm) from the top and seal at once with snap lids and screw bands. Process in a boiling water bath [p. 26] or steam canner for 15 minutes.

Gooseberry-Rhubarb Jam

This jam has a delicious tart flavor and lovely amber color, another reason to freeze tender rhubarb stalks. In this case, stalks of the red type must be cut early in the season before they get stringy.

Makes about 3 pt (1.5L)

1 qt gooseberries (1 L)
1 qt cut-up tender red rhubarb stalks (1 L)
6 cups sugar (1.5 L)
1/2 cup water (125 mL)

Add water to fruit. Cover and bring to simmering. Remove cover, stir in sugar and bring to a rolling boil. Boil about 10 minutes. Fill hot scalded jars [p. 28] to 1/4 inch (5 mm) from the top and seal at once with snap lids and screw bands. Process in a boiling water bath [p. 26] or steam canner for 15 minutes.

Gooseberry Marmalade

THIS IS GUARANTEED TO BE A HIT AMONG THE MOST SOPHISTICATED GOURMETS. ONCE, SOME CUSTOMERS CAME LOOKING FOR CHUTNEY, BUT I DIDN'T HAVE ANY, SO I OFFERED THEM SOME OF MY GOOSEBERRY MARMALADE INSTEAD. THE HUSBAND OF ONE OF THE WOMEN LATER REMARKED, "THEY WENT GAGA OVER IT." USE FIRM RIPENING BERRIES.

Makes 3 to 3 /2 pt (1.5 to 1.75 L)

3 pt gooseberries (3.5 L)
Sugar
2 lemons
1 cup water (250 mL)
4 oranges

Blanch gooseberries by pouring boiling water over them. Drain in a colander.

Peel lemons and oranges. Reserve peel. Slice pulp thinly; add to gooseberries. Turn fruit and sugar into a large stainless-steel pot, using 1 cup (250 mL) sugar to every cup (250 mL) fruit. Stir well. Cover and let stand overnight. Using scissors, cut reserved peel into thin shreds. Place in a bowl and add 1 cup (250 mL) water. Cover and let stand overnight as well.

Add peel-water mixture to fruit. Stirring frequently with a long-handled wooden spoon, simmer, uncovered, for about 1 hour or until mixture thickens.

Remove marmalade from heat and let subside. Stir. Fill hot scalded jars [p. 28] to 1/4 inch (5 mm) from the top and seal with snap lids and screw bands. Process in a boiling-water bath [p. 26] or steam canner for 10 minutes.

Note: Do not increase the amounts because the marmalade may darken and lose its flavor.

Gooseberry Chutney

The original directions called for topping and tailing and halving the gooseberries. Needless to say, these directions don't. Serve chutney with cold meat. Use underripe gooseberries.

Makes 2 to 3 Pt (1 to 1.5 L)

3 lb gooseberries (1.5 kg)
1 oz ginger (30 g)
2 oz salt (50 g)
1 cinnamon stick
1 pt malt vinegar (500 mL)
1 oz mustard seeds (30 g)
2 cups sugar (500 mL)
2 tsp cayenne pepper (10 mL)

Bruise gooseberries with a wooden stamper or mallet or chop them coarsely with a hand chopper. Place in a bowl and sprinkle with salt. Cover and let stand overnight. Drain and rinse.

In a large stainless-steel pot, combine 1/2 pt (250 mL) malt vinegar and sugar. Stirring to dissolve sugar, bring to a boil and simmer until mixture forms a thick syrup. Add remaining vinegar and gooseberries. Simmer, uncovered, for 10 minutes. Add ginger, cinnamon, mustard seeds, and cayenne pepper and, stirring occasionally, simmer for another 30 minutes or until thick. It should be a reddish color, not too dark.

Remove chutney from heat and retrieve cinnamon stick. Pour into hot scalded jars [p. 28], leaving 1/4 inch (5 mm) headroom, and seal immediately with snap lids and screw bands. Process in a boiling-water bath [p. 26] or steam canner for 10 minutes.

Note: 3 lb (1.5 kg) gooseberries equals about 6 *heaping* cups (1.5 L).

Gooseberry-Cream Snow

Serves 2 to 3

2 cups ripe gooseberries (500 mL)
1 cup whipping cream [p. 58] (250 mL)
1/2 cup water (125 mL)
Sugar
1 egg white

In a pot, simmer together gooseberries and water, covered, until berries are tender and pulpy. Remove lid halfway through cooking, stirring as necessary. With a wooden spoon, beat pulp until quite smooth. Add sugar to taste and chill completely.

In a bowl, beat whipping cream until very stiff. In a separate bowl, beat egg white until stiff, adding 1 Tbsp (15 mL) sugar; fold into cream. Beat gooseberry pulp into whipping-cream mixture a little at a time. Chill until ready to serve.

Canned Gooseberries

For variety, add red currants in some form. Use firm ripe berries.

Makes 5 qt (5 L)

Gooseberries

Light syrup:

1 cup sugar (250 mL)
1 cup honey (250 mL)
1 qt water (1 L)

Prepare syrup. In a stainless-steel pot, combine sugar, honey, and water. Stirring to dissolve honey and sugar, bring to a boil. Pour 1/2 cup (125 mL) boiling syrup into each hot scalded jar [p. 28].

Fill each canning jar with gooseberries and shake jar gently so syrup is well distributed over fruit. If necessary, add more syrup to cover gooseberries, leaving 1/2 inch (1 cm) headroom. Adjust lids and process jars in a boiling-water bath [p. 26] or steam canner for 15 minutes.

Note: A single batch of medium syrup yields about 5 cups (1.25 L). Allow about 1/2 to 1 cup (125 mL to 250 mL) syrup to each qt (L) jar. You can substitute another cup (250 mL) sugar for the honey.

Freezing Gooseberries

If you're too busy during the harvest to preserve gooseberries and you want to use them later in pie or any of the recipes below, just put them into a freezer bag or pack them into a freezer container without sugar and freeze.

Gooseberry Pie or Tart

This was a prized New England pie before the gooseberry bush fell out of favor.

1 qt ripe gooseberries (1 L)
1 egg yolk
Unbaked pie shell [p. 46]
3 Tbsp heavy cream (50 mL)
1 cup sugar (250 mL)

Place gooseberries in an unbaked 9-inch (23-cm) pie shell and sprinkle with sugar. Bake in a 350°F (180°C) oven for about 20 minutes.

Meanwhile, in a bowl, lightly beat egg yolk and mix in cream. Drip mixture over baked pie. Return pie to oven for 15 minutes or until cream mixture forms a crust and berries are tender.

Variation: Omit cream and egg. Precook gooseberries with sugar, adding a little water to prevent scorching. Pour into pie shell, and cover with a lattice top. Bake in a 350°F (180°C) oven for 35 minutes or until crust is browned and berries are tender.

Fresh Stewed Gooseberries

Serves 2 to 3

1/2 cup sugar or honey (125 mL)

1 cup water (250 mL)

1 lb ripe gooseberries (500 g)

In a stainless-steel pot, dissolve sugar or honey in water and bring to a boil. Add gooseberries, cover, and simmer for about 15 minutes or until tender. Uncover halfway through cooking. Drain gooseberries, reserving syrup. Reheat syrup and pour over fruit.

Note: Do not overcook or berries will break down.

Gooseberry Ice Cream

WITH ITS PIQUANT FLAVOR, GOOSEBERRY ICE CREAM IS DELICIOUS.

Makes about 3 qt (3 L)

3 1/2 cups green gooseberries (875 mL)

1 1/2 cups sugar (375 mL)

1 qt cream (1 L)

In a pot, combine gooseberries and sugar. Cover and stew, removing lid halfway through cooking. Add more sugar to taste if desired (or use part honey). Put cooked gooseberries through a food mill and let cool.

Meanwhile, in the top of a double boiler, heat cream over a little boiling water. Let cool as well.

In a bowl, combine gooseberries and cream; stir well. Turn mixture into chilled container of hand ice-cream maker and churn until handle is hard to turn. Ripen for 1 to 2 hours in a cool spot, with the container packed in ice and covered with a burlap bag. Or make a smaller amount in an ice cream machine. Review "An Assortment of Basics" [p. 139–146].

Black Currants

I may as well tell you straight away that I am a black-currant fancier, one of a small but growing number of people in North America (the number is higher in Canada than in the United States) who think that the black currant has been unfairly neglected. The black currant shrub's hardiness, immunity to disease, and ability to produce great crops with little or no attention are hard to match. Given suitable growing conditions, the shrubs grow and produce fruit with more vigor than either gooseberry or red currant bushes. Black currant bushes are also beautiful, with their curved branches dipping down to the ground. In early summer, they are crammed with clusters of small greenish-white flowers and then with clusters of ripe black berries.

So why doesn't everyone have a black currant bush in his or her fruit garden? The charges are as follows: black currants are host to white-pine blister rust, black currants have an undesirable flavor, black currants are not worth growing.

Let's take a look at those accusations. Yes, black currants do carry white-pine blister rust, but so do other members of the *Ribes* group (gooseberries and red currants). This fact has not prevented garden writers from promoting gooseberries and red currants, however, and as a result, those fruits are enjoying a modest comeback in the trade. On the other hand, the black currant suffers from bad publicity, often being singled out as the sole culprit of white-pine blister rust, without any further explanation. Therefore I think the following account is in order.

White-pine blister rust was inadvertently brought to North America around the turn of the century, the same time that the white pine was enjoying considerable commercial popularity. In the first stage of its development, the fungus lives on the *Ribes* species, and it does little harm. But in the second stage, it lives inside the stem of the white pine, causing severe damage or death to the tree. By 1918, millions of acres of pine forests were infected by the fungus. At that time, the United Slates government took steps to prohibit the growth and sale of currants and gooseberries. Eventually, the white pine's commercial value declined, and in 1968 the government revoked the quarantine and eased the restrictions against *Ribes* species. Each state then set up its own regulations.

By contrast, Canada, according to some horticulturists, has had a more enlightened policy toward *Ribes.* Though there is no shortage of white pines in Canada, there are no restrictions against currants and gooseberries. Instead, authorities have worked to combat the problem through breeding programs. Perhaps this attitude stems in part from the fact that there is a stronger British tradition there. Indeed, the British are avid fans of *Ribes,* of black currants in particular.

When I was researching the original edition of this book, I decided to investigate state prohibitions against black currants. After all, if Americans were not allowed to grow black currants, what would be the use in telling them how wonderful they are? I was also interested in finding out if United States horticultural officials knew why black currants were pinpointed as the worst offenders against white pines. The more I looked into the matter, the more confused the situation appeared to be. My first inquiries, sent to plant associations and horticultural authorities, drew a blank. Nothing, it seemed, was known about black currants. No one knew if the plants were for sale anywhere in the United States; no one knew if the plants were allowed to be grown. In short, I got the definite feeling that black currants were regarded as pariahs of no horticultural interest.

Then I sent out inquiries to 16 state agricultural research stations and departments of conservation and to the United States Department of Agriculture.

I asked about the status of black currants in their areas, whether or not they were thought to be more susceptible to white-pine blister rust than other *Ribes* species and, finally, whether black currants had a future, and if so, what was it? In no time, I accumulated a rather bulky folder of information. The answers I received, although direct and to the point, were sometimes conflicting.

Maine and New Hampshire, where the white pine was still a viable commercial crop, outlaw black currants, with some restrictions on red currants and gooseberries. Rhode Island and Michigan prohibited the growth and sale of black currants but admittedly did not enforce the laws. (For example, a nursery in Ypsilanti, Michigan, received permission to sell black currant plants because there are not any white pines in that area.) It was generally felt, except in a few instances, that the question of enforcing prohibitions is academic, anyway: wild *Ribes* species grow vigorously and cannot be controlled. Some officials in Alaska noted as well that even though there was no ban in their state, white-pine forests were unaffected. Some officials were adamant that black currants are more susceptible to white-pine blister rust than gooseberries and red currants, while others were just as adamant that all *Ribes* are equally guilty. Many of my respondents, pointing to the inefficacy of past bans and the decline of the white-pine industry, said it was time to revise and review old, outdated laws. Some held out promise for a more lenient attitude toward black currants because of the availability of more effective controls, such as fungicides and disease-resistant varieties.

At the same time that these plant officials voiced differing views, scientists in Canada and individuals in the United States were continuing work to breed varieties resistant to white-pine blister rust, as well as types with bigger fruit and higher yields. The three varieties that still may be the most resistant to white-pine blister (Consort, Crusader, and Cornet) were all developed in Canada, at the Horticultural Research Institute of Ontario, at Vineland Station. Of these, Consort is considered the most resistant. It used to be the most popular and the most widely available in Canada, as well as the United States. In addition, two new varieties from Europe were then being tested in Canada; the Josta, also disease resistant, was developed in Germany. With the continued and growing interest in many "old-fashioned" fruits, there is no doubt that government-run experimental fruit stations in the United States will be moved to conduct similar research.

As for the charge that black currants have an undesirable flavor, I am convinced that most gardening writers in the United States have never tasted black currants in any form. Those few people who do go out of their way to try black currants are well rewarded. The late American gardening writer Lewis Hill once said that he and his wife were "converted to the taste when we bought a jar of 'confiture de cassis,' black-currant jam, in Canada." When I sent Hill a sample of our dried black currants, he was more than enthusiastic: "We are certainly going to expand our production. They are great!" *Update:* The Hills went on to breed and select black currants at their Greensboro, Vermont plant nursery. The variety Hill's Kiev Select is one of Lewis Hill's selections.

What exactly is the flavor of black currants? In 1944, the great American horticulturist U. P. Hedrick said that the black currant has an "assertive flavor and aroma . . . it is most pleasant to eat out of hand or in culinary dishes." Others have called its taste "musky." It is certainly assertive, but I'm not sure about musky. The word *musky* usually carries negative overtones, yet it also describes the appealing scent of many flavors.

To be honest, however, I think that black currants must be processed to be properly appreciated. Gardeners and commercial growers in Europe understand this well, although the British do enjoy a dish of fresh black currants and cream for breakfast. In any case, British children are as familiar with morning glasses of black currant juice as American children are with orange juice. In Europe, black currant is a highly prized flavoring for cordials, liqueurs, wines, desserts, and candies; rum with a shot of black currant syrup, I'm told, makes an incomparable drink.

Finally, are black currants worth growing? If you know nothing about a fruit except that it is a carrier of a dreaded disease (like Typhoid Mary) and tastes funny, you may well conclude that it is not. But if you have ever tasted black currant jam, jelly, wine, juice, or the dried berries, if you have ever seen a bush drooping under the weight of its fruit you will search from one end of the country to the other to find just one rootstock to plant in your garden. If you can find the *real* thing, in whatever form, on the shelves of a specialty shop or in the pages of a British mail-order catalog, you can make up your own mind about the flavor of black currants. And from there, you can decide whether to grow them.

Update: Since I wrote the above, some states have lifted their ban on growing black currants, while others have loosened restrictions in certain counties. Some states confine the planting of black currants to rust-resistant varieties, but the lists vary. The best advice is to consult your local Cooperative Extensive office (see Appendix) to find out about specific restrictions in your area. Although there are more black currant varieties available now than ever before, not all of them are noted for being rust-resistant; some bear larger, sweeter, juicier fruit, are earlier ripening, and may be mildew-resistant. Note that some of the plant nurseries which carry black currant shrubs list states to which they cannot ship plants. On the whole, however, the black currant picture is promising, especially since the fruits' health benefits have been publicized. Not only do black currants possess a high level of Vitamin C, the fruit has been found to be a rich source of potassium, phosphorous, iron, and other nutrients, and is high in antioxidants. It has, in fact, been described as the ultimate "superfruit" that may help fight cancer, heart disease, and Alzheimer's. With this kind of profile, surely it will not be long before black currants will be safer to grow throughout the country.

Planting

If there are white pines in your area or on your property, plant black currant rootstocks 1000 ft (300 m) from the stands of the trees.

In northern climates, plant black currant shrubs in the spring. One bush is more than enough for one person—the yield is enormous (2 gallons/8 L or more). We have six bushes, and we never calculate our yield. We are too busy picking quart after quart. The best site for black currants is a slope with a northern exposure to provide cool conditions. As long as the soil provides sufficient drainage for the roots, the particular type is not too important because it can be changed to suit the plant. As with other *Ribes,* though, fertile clay loam is best.

To plant, trim plants to 4 to 6 inches (10 to 15 cm) and put them in a bucket of water while preparing holes. With a spade, make holes every 6 ft (2 m), 1 ft (30 cm) more than for red currants or gooseberries, in rows about 6 to 10 ft (2 to 3 m) apart. It's hard to believe, but in two or three years each small plant will mature into a candelabra of spreading branches. The tips of the branches may eventually touch, but that's okay. Just trim the offending branches whenever necessary.

If you have limited space, consider growing them, as well as gooseberries and red currants, in espalier form where branches are trained to grow on wires and supports, either against a wall or standing alone. But although production is great, maintenance is a lot of work, what with frequent tying, pinching, and pruning. But they are very attractive grown that way.

Add a shovelful of well-rotted compost to each hole and water it. Build a little mound of earth and set the roots over it, tamping the soil well around the plant. In a dry spell, water the plants regularly until they show signs of new growth.

Cultivating

Black currant bushes benefit from mulching as do other *Ribes.* Mulch keeps the plants cool, prevents weeds, and ultimately breaks down, adding organic matter to the soil. As already noted, we prefer a mulch that consists of three layers: manure or well-rotted compost; heavy paper, cardboard, or worn-out nonsynthetic carpet; hay, straw, or if you live close to a shore, eel grass. Whatever materials you use for mulch, it should be set down in a 2-ft (60-cm) wide ring around the plant, and it should be renewed once a year, in spring or fall.

When the plants are dormant, in early spring, remove dead and broken stems. Thin out vigorous shrubs that are more than three years old so that the center of the plant is not overcrowded. A dozen branches, a mix of one-, two-, and three-year-old ones, will provide more than enough berries if the growing conditions are satisfactory.

You will not need to worry about propagating black currant shrubs if their site provides them with cool conditions, adequate drainage, and fertile soil. They will reproduce themselves by self-layering—and much more vigorously than red currant plants. Make cuttings from the layered branches and plant them fairly close together in a nursery bed for one season before moving them to a permanent location. Remember, plant them in friable soil; weed and water them during the growing season as needed.

Harvesting

Harvesting black currants is an acquired art; it can start in late July and continue through August. Have a plan such as the following.

First, pick slightly underripe black currants for jelly. These berries, still a bit green, can be harvested quickly, as the stems can be left on. Second, pick the slightly riper, mostly black berries for jam, free of stems. You can wait several days between pickings, but do not wait too long—the birds may beat you to it. Third, pick the dead-ripe berries for juice. If you intend to make juice as a byproduct of making dried berries, pick those berries free of stems. If you want to make wine or mead or some other beverage, use dead-ripe currants as well, leaving on the stems.

Preserving, Canning, Freezing, And Cooking

There are few fruits so ill-served by modern cookbooks as black currants, but considering their history of neglect, this is not surprising. You may find a recipe for black currant jam, but more than likely the directions will be unnecessarily complicated, requiring a great deal of chopping and cooking and even the use of a food processor. Or the addition of commercial pectin, which seems excessive with a fruit so high in natural pectin and so quick setting.

The following recipes, our favorites over the years, have been gleaned from old cookbooks or adapted from other recipes. The procedure for jelly and jam making has been streamlined to reflect the general principles outlined in chapter one. It's hard to advise you what to do with your crop—the jam, jelly, juice, wine, and dried berries are all wonderful. But in cooking, dried black currants and black currant wine are particularly versatile. Dried currants are a nice addition to cookies and buns; black currant wine is suitable for chicken or beef dishes. Review A Short Course in Fruit Preserving [p. 3–14] before preserving.

Black Currant Jelly

After you have made this great jelly once, you will wonder why commercial black currant jelly often contains artificial coloring. Try this jelly with cream cheese and bread. Use a mixture of ripe and underripe black currants.

1 qt (1 L) juice makes about 2 pt (1 L)

Black currants with stems
Sugar

In a large preserving pot, cover at least 2 qt (2 L) black currants with water. Cover and boil until currants are soft, occasionally crushing fruit with a large wooden spoon, mallet, or paddle. Strain mixture through a jelly bag [p. 28] and let drip for several hours or overnight. Reserve juice.

Bring pulp to a boil again and strain through a jelly bag, letting drip until dry.

Combine juice from both extractions. Measure juice and cook 4 cups at a time in a large stainless-steel pot. Cover and bring to a boil. Stir in 1 cup (250 mL) sugar to each cup (250 mL) juice. Bring to a rolling boil. Skimming as necessary, boil, uncovered, for about 15 minutes or less or until a small amount sheets off a metal spoon [p. 28-29].

Remove jelly from heat and let subside. Stir, skimming if desired. Fill hot scalded jars [p. 28] to 1/4 inch (5 mm) from the top and seal at once with snap lids and screw bands. Process in a boiling-water bath [p. 26] or steam canner for 10 minutes.

Black Currant Jam

This is a fast-setting jam. Use just-ripe black currants, with some slightly underripe.

Makes 1 1/2 to 2 pt (750 mL to 1 L)

4 cups black currants without stems (1 L)
3 cups sugar (750 mL)
1/2 cup water or grape juice (125 mL)

In a large stainless-steel pot, combine black currants and liquid. Mash if desired. Cover and bring to a boil. Stir in sugar and bring to a boil again. Reduce heat slightly. Stirring occasionally, cook, uncovered, for about 10 minutes or until mixture thickens and begins to cling to bottom of pot.

Remove jam from heat and let subside. Stir, skimming if desired. Fill hot scalded jars [p. 28] to 1/4 inch (5 mm) from the top and seal at once with snap lids and screw bands. Process in a boiling-water bath [p. 26] or steam canner for 15 minutes.

Cottage Cheese

To make cream cheese, you have to make cottage cheese first. Find a gallon or two of unpasteurized milk, preferably from a Jersey cow. With cottage cheese, practice makes perfect. Don't go the rennet route: you will be disappointed with the bland product.

Makes about 1 qt (1 L)

1 gallon unpasteurized milk (4 L)
Cream
Salt

Pour unpasteurized milk into a large preserving pot. Cover and let stand in a warm place until milk forms a solid gelatinous mass similar to junket or custard, about 24 to 48 hours. To test, tip pot slightly to see if curd slides up side of pot. If so, it is ready for heating.

Set pot over low heat or in a large pan of hot water and gently break up curd by hand until it is uniform. Continue to heat slowly and stir until curds are fairly firm pieces and are separated from whey (curds are white and whey is yellowish). When curds are sufficiently firm, the mixture will probably be as hot as your hand can stand.

Remove curds from heat and drain through a large cheesecloth bag [see Jelly Bag, p. 28]. Let drip overnight.

Break up curds with a slotted spoon or a fork. Stir in cream and salt to taste. Place cottage cheese in a plastic container and chill thoroughly. If curds are grainy and hard, mixture was overcooked. If curds are soft, mixture was undercooked, and cottage cheese will sour quickly.

Note: To hasten the initial thickening process, add 1/2 cup (125 mL) buttermilk.

Cream Cheese

To make cream cheese, follow the recipe for cottage cheese through to draining the curds overnight and proceed.

Makes 1 qt (1 L)

1 qt dry curds (1 L)
1 cup heavy cream (250 mL)
1 /4 cup butter (50 mL)
1 1/2 scant tsp salt (7 mL)
1/2 tsp baking soda (2 mL)

Place dry curds in the top of a double boiler. With your hands, work butter into curds. Add baking soda. Place mixture over bottom of double boiler, making sure water does not touch top pot. Add some of cream to curds. Stirring occasionally and adding more cream if dry, slowly heat mixture for 10 minutes or until it turns gummy and sticky. As you stir, gummy strands will begin to form on bottom of pot.

Remove pot from heat and stir in remaining cream or enough to make a thick mixture the consistency of pudding. Stir in salt. Place cream cheese in a plastic container and refrigerate for several hours before using.

Note: Do not worry if cream cheese is not completely smooth, as little lumps will eventually dissolve.

Dried Black Currants

These look like small dark raisins. Dried currants should still have a tender, slightly moist quality, but they should not be sticky. Use dead-ripe black currants.

Makes about 1 lb (500 g)

3 cups black currants without stems (750 mL)
1 cup sugar (250 mL)

Layer black currants and sugar consecutively in a medium-sized preserving pot. Cover and let stand overnight to draw out juices.

Bring mixture to a boil. Reduce heat and, stirring occasionally, simmer gently for 15 minutes. Strain black currants and reserve juice.

Place currants on trays lined with heavy brown paper and spread them out evenly. Set trays in direct sunlight. Stir currants daily to prevent sticking. After first day of drying, change paper. Drying takes about 3 to 4 days, depending on weather.

Note: This recipe can be used to dry blueberries as well.

Black Currant Juice

VERY SIMILAR TO THE BRITISH PRODUCT, RIBENA, A BLACK CURRANT JUICE CONCENTRATE.

To make juice, bring reserved juice from making dried currants to a boil and simmer for about 5 minutes. Pour into hot scalded jars [p. 28], leaving 1/2 inch (1 cm) headroom, and seal at once with snap lids and screw bands. Process in a boiling-water bath [p. 26] or steam canner for 15 minutes. To use, add 3 qt (3 L) water to 1 qt (1 L) syrup.

Variation: To make Black Currant Juice without first making berries, add 1 cup sugar (250 mL) to 1 quart (1 L) fruit. Let sit to bring out juices. Stir, bring to a boil, simmer 10 minutes and pour into hot scalded jars [p. 28], leaving 1/2 inch (1 cm) headroom, and seal at once with snap lids and screw bands. Process in a boiling-water bath [p. 26] or steam canner for 15 minutes. To use, dilute with water to taste.

Black Currant Wine

This is one of the best homemade wines. Use it as a substitute in any recipe calling for red wine, such as coq au vin. Of course, it's grand to serve with spaghetti or a special meal. Use clean dead-ripe or overripe black currants with or without stems.

Black currants
Sugar
Juice of 1 lemon or 2 Tbsp sugar
(25 mL) REAL Lemon
Wine or baking yeast

In a large preserving pot, cover black currants with water, using as much fruit as desired. Make about 5 to 10 extractions as for black currant jelly (p. 76), until pulp loses color.

Combine and measure liquid from extractions. Place in a large crock or plastic bucket. Stir in 2 lb (1 kg) sugar to each gallon (4 L) juice and mix in lemon juice.

Dissolve 1 Tbsp (15 mL) yeast in a little warm water and add to liquid. Stir mixture again and cover container. Let mixture ferment at 70° to 75°F (20° to 25°C) for 10 days.

Siphon contents into glass jugs, using cotton plugs as stoppers. Store wine at 60° to 65°F (15° to 18°C), away from direct sunlight, which could ruin the nice ruby color. When wine stops bubbling completely (in about 1 month), resiphon into permanent bottles. Seal and store in a cool, dark, dry place. If using corks, store bottles lying down.

Note: If you do not make multiple extractions, the juice will be too strong and will make an unpalatable wine. Besides, you can make a lot of wine from a small amount of currants.

Crème de Cassis

FRIEND AND FRUIT MAVIN, LOIS ROSE, HAS BEEN MAKING THIS ANCIENT FRENCH LIQUEUR FOR ALMOST 20 YEARS, ADAPTED FROM JANE GRIGSON'S *JANE GRIGSON'S FRUIT BOOK*. THE CONSISTENCY, AS THE NAME IMPLIES, SHOULD BE CREAMY, ALTHOUGH THERE'S NO CREAM IN IT. THERE ARE MANY WAYS TO USE CRÈME DE CASSIS BESIDES SIPPING IT SLOWLY OR MIXING INTO COCKTAILS. TRY OVER VANILLA ICE CREAM.

2 lb black currants (1 kg)
4 full cups red wine (1 L)
3 lb sugar (1 ½ kg)
1 1/2 pt brandy, gin, or vodka (700 mL)

Soak fruit in wine for 48 hours. Place several layers of fine cheesecloth over a pot. Process currants and wine in a blender until mush and pour into cheesecloth to drain. Pull ends together and twist hard to squeeze out all the liquid you can. Pour resulting juice into a pot, add sugar and stir at a very low heat for 2 hours until the juice is reduced a bit. Overheating can spoil the cassis, giving it a cooked taste (Lois uses a heat disperser under the cooking pot). The idea is to cook at a low enough temperature, above blood heat and lower than simmering, to reduce the liquid without evaporating all the alcohol. You really have to stick with it, stirring at intervals during the 2 hours. Cool, then add 3 parts juice to 1 part brandy, gin, or 151 vodka and bottle. Let sit a few months before opening.

New Year's Punch for 20

Drink straight or mixed with fruit juice and ice for a great summer drink.

5 gallons lukewarm water (20 L)
1 Tbsp cream of tartar (25 mL)
3 3/4 lb sugar (2.75 kg)
2 lemons
3/4 oz ginger (20 g)
1/2 tsp baking yeast (2 mL)

Place water in a large crock or pot, stir in sugar, ginger, and cream of tartar.

Cut lemons into thin slices and add to water mixture. Dissolve yeast in a little warm water; add to liquid. Stir, cover, and let stand overnight.

Siphon ginger ale into soda bottles and cap with a hand capper. Ready to use in 5 days. Store in a cool, dark, dry place.

Black Mead

Mead is an ancient drink made by fermenting honey with other ingredients. Let this drink age for at least a year—it's worth the wait. Use clean dead-ripe or overripe black currants with or without stems.

Makes 1 gallon (4 L)

4 lb black currants (2 kg)
Juice of 2 lemons
2 lb honey (1 kg)
4 green apples, chopped
6 pt warm water (3 L)
1 Tbsp wine or baking yeast (15 mL)
1/4 tsp Marmite (1 mL)
1 Tbsp strong tea (15 mL)
Cold water

In a large preserving pot, crush black currants with a wooden spoon or mallet.

In a bowl, dissolve honey in warm water. Add Marmite, tea, lemon juice, and apples. Dissolve yeast in warm water. Add honey-apple mixture and yeast to crushed black currants. Stir, cover, and let stand for 3 days.

Strain, pressing pulp slightly. Add enough cold water to make 1 gallon (4 L) liquid. Cover and let ferment at 70° to 75°F (20° to 25°C) for 10 days. Siphon contents into glass jugs, using cotton plugs as stoppers. Store mead at 60° to 65°F (15° to 18°C), away from direct sunlight. When mead stops bubbling completely, resiphon into permanent bottles. Store in a cool, dark, dry place. If sealed with corks, store bottles lying down.

Coq au Vin

Serves 4

3 1/2 lb frying chicken, cut up (1.75 kg)
Bacon drippings
Salt
Pepper
1/2 lb small onions, cut up (250 g)
1/2 lb fresh mushrooms or a good handful of dried (250 g)
2 Tbsp flour (25 ml)
2 cups black currant wine [p. 79] (500 ml)
1 large clove garlic, minced
2 to 3 shallots or ½ cup (125 mL) chopped onions or scallions
Several sprigs fresh parsley, chopped, or a few pinches of dried
1/4 tsp thyme (1 ml)
1/2 bay leaf

In a large frying pan, sauté chicken in bacon drippings, adding salt and pepper to taste. When chicken is browned on both sides, place in a roasting pan. Place in a 350°F (180°C) oven to await sauce.

Sauté onions and mushrooms in chicken-bacon fat. When onions begin to brown, remove pan from heat, stir in flour, return to heat, and gradually stir in wine. Add garlic, shallots, parsley, thyme, and bay leaf. Stirring constantly, simmer sauce for 1 to 2 minutes, adding more liquid (wine or water) as desired.

Remove chicken from oven. Pour sauce over chicken, cover, and continue baking for about 1 hour or until chicken is tender. While baking, baste occasionally, and before done, remove cover to brown. Serve with rice and more black currant wine.

Note: If using dried mushrooms, presoak them in boiling water for about 10 minutes and drain, reserving liquid to add to wine.

Black Currant Sticky Buns

Makes 3 dozen

1/4 tsp ginger (1 mL)
1 cup dried currants (p. 108) or a mixture of part raisins (250 mL)
1 tsp granulated sugar (5 mL)
1 Tbsp dry yeast (15 mL)
1/2 cup warm water (125 mL)
Cinnamon (for mixing into dough)
Melted butter
Sugar-cinnamon mix (to taste)
1 cup milk (250 mL)
1/2 cup shortening (125 mL)
1/3 cup honey (75 mL)
1 tsp salt (5 mL)

Syrup:

1 cup cold water (250 mL)
3 Tbsp butter (50 mL)
1 egg, well beaten
2 cups brown sugar (500 mL)
12 cups flour (part whole-wheat) (3 L)
2 Tbsp water (25 mL)

In a large bowl, sprinkle ginger, 1 tsp (5 mL) granulated sugar, and yeast on warm water. Let stand undisturbed until foaming.

In a saucepan, scald milk and melt in shortening. Stir in honey and salt. Remove from heat. Stir in cold water to cool mixture to warm. Add milk mixture to dissolved yeast; stir well. Add well-beaten egg and stir in a few cups of flour, beating well. Add currants. Mix in more flour until dough is stiff enough to knead.

Knead dough and when almost finished, sprinkle cinnamon on all sides and knead in. Cover bowl with a cloth and let dough rise in a warm place until doubled in size.

Meanwhile, prepare syrup. In an 11-inch (3.5-L) skillet, melt 3 Tbsp (50 mL) butter, add enough brown sugar to cover bottom of pan, and add 2 Tbsp (25 mL) water. (Add more brown sugar if you want stickier buns.) Bring mixture to a boil and cook for a few minutes. Pour onto 2 cookie sheets, tilting pans so they are evenly coated.

Divide dough into thirds. Roll out each piece into a rectangle about 1/4 inch (5 mm) thick. Spread each with melted butter and sprinkle with a little sugar-cinnamon mix. Roll up each piece longways and cut into buns 1 1/2 inches (4 cm) wide. Place buns, cut side down, on cookie sheets. Cover with a towel and let stand until dough begins to rise. Bake in a 350°F (180°C) oven for about 15 minutes. Remove to a platter immediately, flipping each bun so sticky side is up.

Jellyroll with Black Currant Jam

4 eggs, separated
1/2 tsp salt (2 mL)
3/4 cup sifted sugar (175 mL)
Icing sugar
1 tsp vanilla (5 mL)
Black currant jam [p. 107] or jelly [p. 106]
3/4 cup cake flour (175 mL)
3/4 tsp baking powder (4 mL)

In a bowl, beat egg yolks until light. Gradually add sifted sugar and beat mixture until creamy. Add vanilla.

Sift together flour, baking powder, and salt. Gradually add to sugar-egg yolk mixture. Beat until smooth. In a separate bowl, beat egg whites until stiff; fold into batter.

Grease a shallow 7-inch x 11 -inch (2-L) baking pan and line it with wax paper. Pour in batter and bake in a 375° F (190°C) oven for 12 to 15 minutes.

Remove cake from oven and flop onto a dish towel well sprinkled with icing sugar. Trim off any hard edges, then roll up cake in towel. When ready to use, unroll and spread at least 1/2 cup (125 mL) black currant jam or desired amount over top of cake. Roll up cake, jam side in, wrap towel around it, and let sit for about 15 minutes before slicing and serving.

Variation: Make your favorite sponge cake and cut into 2 layers. Thickly cover top of bottom layer with black currant jam. Add top layer and spread with whipped cream [p. 58]. Chill before serving.

Black Currant-Leaf Cream

I learned about this dish from a friend who is a fine gardener and cook. It is wonderfully refreshing in the heat of summer and can be used to great effect to top parfaits, ice cream, and sorbets. When cooking the leaves you can toss in a small handful of berries for extra black currant flavor.

Serves 4

1 cup young black currant leaves (250 mL)
2 egg whites
1 cup whipped cream [p. 58] (250 mL)
2 cups sugar (500 mL)
1 cup water (250 mL)
Touch lemon juice

In a pot, boil together black currant leaves, sugar, and water for 15 minutes, stirring to dissolve sugar. Strain, reserving syrup.

In a bowl, beat egg whites until stiff. *Gently* pour hot syrup onto egg whites. Beat until mixture begins to thicken. Let cool.

Fold whipped cream and lemon juice into cooled mixture. Spoon into individual bowls and chill.

Boodle's Fool

Serves 6

3 cups black or red currants or gooseberries (750 mL)
1 pt whipping cream [p. 58] (500 mL)
Sugar or honey
1 stale cake, broken up, or equivalent amount of cookies

Prepare juice. In a large pot, combine about 3 cups (750 mL) ripe black currants with a little water. Cover and bring to a boil. Boil until currants are soft, occasionally crushing fruit with a large wooden spoon, mallet, or paddle. Strain mixture through a jelly bag [p. 28] and let drip for several hours or overnight. Measure 1 cup (250 mL.) juice. Sweeten juice to taste with honey or sugar.

In a bowl, beat whipping cream halfway to stiff and add currant juice. Continue beating until mixture is frothy. Pour mixture over broken-up pieces of cake or over cookies. Chill for at least 4 hours.

Black Currant Sorbet/Ice

This dessert is bound to impress. It is not only delicious and cooling, but a lovely rosy pink, especially beautiful when served in parfait glasses, topped with whipped cream or black currant leaf cream and embellished with an edible flower. I like to use zebrina mallow (*Malva sylvestris zebrina*), a small to medium sized soft pink trumpet with purple stripes, like a miniature hollyhock. Review "An Assortment of Basics" [p.120] for using an ice cream machine.

Makes a little more than 1 qt (1 L)

2 cups unsweetened black currant juice from extraction 500 mL
1 cup water 250 mL
2 cups sugar 500 mL

Pre-mix juice and sugar in ice cream machine canister, cover with freezing cover and chill for faster freezing. When ready to begin freezing, turn on the machine, set canister in ice bucket, pour in water and layer ice and salt as directed. Remove freezing cover, insert paddle, and put mixing cover in place, adding more water according to directions. Turn on machine and add more salt and ice as directed when ice begins to melt. Continue freezing until sorbet is the consistency you want. This should take about 12-20 minutes. Remove canister, check sorbet and stir if needed, store in freezer for an hour or more, then you may remove sorbet to a plastic freezer container and return to freezer.

Variation: Substitute unsweetened red currant juice, or any unsweetened fruit juice, and proceed.

Elderberries

The elderberry often occupied a favored spot in the old-fashioned fruit garden—perhaps a corner where it could grow undisturbed, its branches spreading to 8 ft (2.5 m) when laden with fruit, the plant itself growing about 12 ft (4 m) under good conditions. In early July, the glorious elderblossoms, or elderblow, were picked for wine and jelly making. The buds were pickled, the florets were shaken into pancake and muffin batters to lighten and sweeten them. Later in the season, before the first frosts of autumn, the clusters of shiny purple-black fruit were picked mainly for wine making, although elderberry jelly and pie were also looked on with great favor. The experienced cook knew just where to find the hard sour green apples that, when combined with elderberries, made a firm, flavorful jelly. (Unlike many other small fruits, elderberries do not contain much natural pectin.) Large trays of ripe elderberries were set out in the sun to dry so that elderberry pie could be enjoyed throughout the winter.

When the creamy white umbels of elderflowers bloom, as giant saucers, they seem to embody the characteristics of summer—long sweet-scented sunny days. Then later, some time before the first frost, the ripening clusters of dark berries remind us that shorter days, cold nights, and the end of the growing season are close at hand. Even If you never harvest a single flower or berry, you may enjoy growing the elderberry bush just to look at it.

Sambuccus canadensis, the elderberry of the old-fashioned fruit garden, grows wild in thickets all across Canada and the United States. Beware, though. If you gather elderberries in the wild, do not confuse the purple-black berry with the red variety, *Sambuccus pubens,* which blossoms and fruits earlier. The red berries, reputedly, are inedible, though birds do enjoy them.

Luckily, cultivated elderberries, including European varieties (*S. nigra*) and ornamental types that bear significantly, are widely available from plant nurseries. There are several ornamental varieties in my garden that are wonderful landscaping shrubs, including Black Lace (with pink flowers) and golden elderberry, a heavy bearer. Modern breeding has made elderberries even more attractive for preserving by enlarging the berries and shortening the ripening time of some varieties—Nova, for example. Elderberries are hardy, easy to grow, and adaptable to a wide range of soils and growing conditions. If you have the space, they certainly deserve to be grown in your fruit garden. High in Vitamin C, the berries' reputed health benefits are similar to black currants.

Planting

Elderberries thrive best in fertile, moist, and loamy soil. If your soil is heavy, try to plant rootstocks on a slope, preferably one with a southern exposure. If you can devote a whole southern-facing bank to the planting, the reward at blossom time will more than pay for the space. A slope will not only provide perfect drainage, but will help shelter the plants from early frost—important with later-ripening elderberries—and diseases such as mildew. Plant two varieties for best pollination. Nova, introduced in 1960 by the Agriculture Canada Experiment Station in Kentville, Nova Scotia, is often planted with York, a cultivar with extra large berries and also developed in Canada.

To plant, use a sharp spade and dig holes deep enough to receive the roots of the elderberry stock. Space the plants at least 6 ft (2 m) apart, with 8 to 10 ft (2.5 to 3 m) between rows. It is important not to let the roots dry out, so submerge them in a bucket of water until all the plants are set in the holes. Water each hole, place the plant in the center, spreading out the roots. Fill and cover the hole with soil and tamp the earth firmly into place. Water again, slowly. Next, lay down a 2-ft (60-cm) wide ring of mulch around the base of the plant: a thick layer of compost or manure; a layer of paper, cardboard, old nonsynthetic carpet, or cloth grain bags; and a thick top layer of straw or rotted sawdust. Once the elderberry plant is well established, in two or three years, the mulch need not be renewed if the soil is fairly fertile.

Cultivating

The only thing to do after mulching is to make sure the young plants receive enough water, particularly at fruiting time. If it is especially dry in late summer or early fall, water the bush to ensure good production.

Elderberry bushes will propagate themselves by sending up shoots outside the ring of the original plant. Allow the original plant to spread in a 2-ft (60-cm) circle, then remove all shoots that grow outside this area. Dig down with a sharp spade to remove the new stem and part of the old root and replant it in a nursery bed or in its permanent place, making sure the soil has adequate drainage. Early each spring, remove dead and winter-damaged stalks on all bushes.

Harvesting

If you want to harvest the blossoms for wine, jelly, or cooking, choose umbels in which most of the florets are newly opened; the flowers on mature umbels shatter easily. Cut the stalks with scissors, and store the flowering umbels with their stalks in a plastic bag in the refrigerator until you are ready to use them.

There is only one important thing to say about harvesting the berries: watch out for the birds! In September, gathering for their journey south, they will be eager to fill up on your elderberries. Netting is the most effective way to keep away birds—if used properly. Plastic or nylon netting is good because it is sturdy and can be reused. Cheesecloth is more effective, however, because the mesh is smaller. Follow the manufacturer's instructions when setting out nets, but do not try to cover too great an area with one net. It is better to concentrate on the best-producing shrubs. Let the birds have the berries from the lesser-producing ones. Several mature shrubs will provide an abundant crop, thousands and thousands of berries.

Check elderberry clusters every day. The berries on each cluster do not all ripen at once, so choose clusters in which most of the berries have ripened. Cut them off with scissors, leaving some stalk, as with harvesting the flowers; the stalks of really ripe fruit break off easily. Hint: it's easier to separate berries from stem if you freeze clusters and pull off the berries while the fruit is still very cold.

Preserving, Canning, Freezing, And Cooking

Use fresh flowers for wine, deep-fry fresh flowers dipped in batter, or shake the florets into pancake or bread batters to lighten and flavor them (and be sure to pick fresh flowers for adding to gooseberries for jelly [p. 72]. Dry flowers for tea. The first ripe berries should go into jelly because the earlier the apples are harvested for elderberry jelly, the better. Turn later berries into jam, preserves, wine, juice, or dried berries. As you will notice, elderberries are invariably coupled with another flavor. Alone, the elderberry, grapelike in flavor, tends to be insipid, so it needs a complement, usually something tart, such as apples, lemons, or vinegar.

Use dried elderberries and elderberry preserves in pies; elderberry juice makes an interesting custard pie. Don't forget to use elderberry wine in cooking wherever red wine is called for. Review A Short Course in Fruit Preserving [p. 4] before preserving.

Elderflower Wine

This is made with the blow, or blossoms, after most of the green stalks have been removed. It is a clear white wine, rather heady and fragrant.

Makes 1 gallon (4 L)

2 qt elderflowers (2 L)
Juice of 2 lemons
1 gallon boiling water (4 L)
2 1/2 lb sugar 1.25 kg)
1 oz wine or baking yeast (30 g)
1 yeast-nutrient tablet
or 1 Tbsp Marmite (15 mL)

Place newly opened elderflowers in a large container and pour boiling water over them. Let mixture steep, covered, 2 to 3 days.

Dissolve yeast in a little warm water. Strain elderflower mixture and add lemon juice, sugar, yeast, and yeast nutrient or Marmite to liquid. Stir, cover, and let ferment at 70° to 75°F (20° to 25°C) for a week.

Siphon into jars, plug with cotton, and store away from light. Resiphon after 3 months and again when wine is done (when all bubbling ceases), at which time jars can be capped and stored in a cool, dark, dry place. If bottles are corked, store lying down.

Dried Elderflowers

You may want to try your hand at drying these glorious flowers to use for winter teas. The trick is quick drying to prevent the flowers from turning brown. You have done a good job if the florets have retained their creamy white color.

Gently shake newly opened elder florets loose from their clusters. Set them in a shallow pan immediately and dry them in a warm oven just after heat has been turned off. Check frequently, gently stirring flowers with a long-handled fork.

Remove dried florets from the oven as soon as they look and feel dry and crisp. Let cool completely in pan before storing in a jar—away from light.

Eldeberry Jelly With Added Pectin

Elderberries need added pectin, whether from apples, crabapples, or from commercial pectin. If you can't find tart apples or crabapples, don't despair. This jelly, made with traditional pectin crystals, is not overly sweet. I followed the amounts and boiling time from Billy Joe Tatum, who did not fail me. Read about pectins [p. 28].

Makes about 3 pt (1.5L)

3 3/4 cups elderberry juice (875.38 mL), extracted from 3-4 lb fruit (1.5-2 kg)
1/4 cup lemon juice (50 mL)
1 box pectin crystals
1/2 tsp butter (2 mL)
5 cups sugar (1.182 L)

Crush fruit, heat and simmer for 15 minutes, strain. Stir pectin into juice until dissolved. Add lemon juice, butter (to prevent boiling over), and bring to a rolling boil that can't be stirred down. Stir in sugar, bring back to a boil and boil hard for 2 minutes. Let mixture subside, skim if necessary. Fill hot scalded jars [p. 28] to 1/4 inch (5 mm) from the top and seal at once with snap lids and screw bands, and seal. Process in a boiling-water bath [p. 26] or steam canner for 10 minutes.

Note: I have not tried commercial pectin with the recipes below. You may be able to adapt them, especially with the low or no sugar needed types.

Elderberry-Apple Jelly

If some stems remain on the elderberries, use heaping amounts.

Makes about 2 pt (1 L)

3 lb tart apples or crabapples (1.5 kg)
1 qt water (1 L)
Sugar
2 qt elderberries (2 L)

Cut up apples. In a large preserving pot, combine apples, early ripe elderberries, and water. Cover and simmer until fruit is very soft, stirring occasionally and mashing when mixture starts to bubble. Strain through a jelly bag [p. 28] and let drip overnight.

Measure juice and cook 4 cups (1 L) at a time in a large stainless-steel pot. Cover and bring to a boil. Stir in 1 cup (250 mL) sugar to each cup (250 mL) juice. Bring to a rolling boil and, skimming as necessary, boil, uncovered, for 10 to 15 minutes or until a small amount sheets off a metal spoon [p. 28-29].

Remove jelly from heat and let subside. Stir, skimming if desired. Process in a boiling-water bath [p. 26] or steam canner for 10 minutes.

Variations: To make *elderberry-orange jelly,* put peel from 1 orange and half a stick of cinnamon in a small cheesecloth bag. Drop spice bag into elderberry-apple juice after sugar has been added. Remove it from pot just before jelly is poured into jars. Process as for Elderberry Jelly.

Elderberry sass is a direct variant of elderberry-apple jelly and is our favorite pancake topping just after maple syrup. Simmer fruit as for jelly, but when cooking juice, add only 2 to 3 cups (500 to 750 mL) sugar to 1 qt (1 L) juice (you can cook more than 4 cups/1 L juice at a time). Boil mixture until it is reduced by one-third or one-quarter. Fill hot scalded jars [p. 28] to 1/2 inch (1 cm) from the top and seal at once with snap lids and screw bands. Process in a boiling water-bath [p. 26] or steam canner for 15 minutes.

Spiced Elderberry Jelly

Makes about 4 1/2 pt (2.25 L)

6 lb tart fresh apples 3 kg

1 Tbsp ground cloves (or 1/4 cup/50 mL whole cloves) (25 mL)

4 qt elderberries with stems (4 L)

1 qt cider vinegar (1 L)

1 qt water (2 L)

Sugar

1 Tbsp ground cinnamon (or 1 /4 cup/50 mL cinnamon stick) (25 mL)

Cut up apples. In a large preserving pot, combine early ripe elderberries, apples, cider vinegar, and water. Simmer, covered, until fruit is soft, stirring as needed. Mash fruit. Strain mixture through a jelly bag [p. 28] and let drip for several hours or overnight

Measure juice and cook 4 cups (1 L) at a time in a large stainless-steel pot. Cover, bring to a boil, and stir in cinnamon and cloves (if whole, put them in a cheesecloth bag). Stir in 1 cup (250 mL) sugar to each cup (250 mL) juice. Boil, uncovered, for 15 minutes or until a small amount sheets off a metal spoon [p. 28-29]. Remove spice bag.

Remove jelly from heat and let subside. Stir, skimming if desired. Fill hot scalded jars [p. 28] to 1/4 inch (5 mm) from the top and seal at once with snap lids and screw bands. Process in a boiling-water bath [p. 26] or steam canner for 10 minutes.

Elderberry-Green Grape Jelly

Makes 2 to 3 pt (1 to 1.5 L)

2 qt elderberries (2 L)

4 cups water (1 L)

2 qt green grapes (2 L)

Sugar

Place early ripe elderberries and ripe green grapes in separate preserving pots. Add 2 cups (500 mL) water to each pot, cover, and simmer until fruit is soft. Strain each mixture through its own jelly bag [p. 28] and let drip overnight.

Combine juice from each receiving pot and measure. Cook 4 cups (1 L) juice at a time in a large stainless-steel pot. Cover and bring to a boil. Stir in 1 cup (250 mL) sugar to each cup (250 mL) juice. Bring to a boil again. Skimming as necessary, boil, uncovered, until a small amount sheets off a metal spoon [p. 28-29].

Remove jelly from heat and let subside. Stir, skimming if desired. Fill hot scalded jars [p. 28] to 1/4 inch (5 mm) from the top and seal at once with snap lids and screw bands. Process in a boiling-water bath [p. 26] or steam canner for 10 minutes.

Elderberry Jam

Lemon and apple juice are acidic and help jelling. You could also use sumac juice [p. 181]. Use later-ripening elderberries.

Makes about 1 1/2 pt (750 mL)

Juice of 2 lemons

1 lb elderberries without stems (500 g)

1/2 cup apple juice (125 mL)

2 cups sugar (500 mL)

In a large stainless-steel pot, combine lemon and apple juice or apple pectin, and elderberries. Mash if desired. Bring to a boil, covered, and stir in sugar. Stirring frequently, boil, uncovered, 10 to 15 minutes or until mixture thickens and begins to cling to bottom of pot.

Remove jam from heat and let subside. Stir, skimming if desired. Fill hot scalded jars [p. 28] to 1/4 inch (5 mm) from the top and seal at once with snap lids and screw bands. Process in a boiling-water bath [p. 26] or steam canner for 15 minutes.

Note: If you like, put cooked elderberries through a food mill before adding sugar.

Elderberry Preserves

Before refrigeration, old-timers used to pour these preserves into a crock, then store, covered, in a cool cellar. Use later-ripening elderberries.

Makes 2 1/2 pt (1.25 L)

8 cups elderberries without stems (2 L)

1 pt vinegar (500 mL)

8 cups sugar (2 L)

In a large stainless-steel pot, combine elderberries, vinegar, and sugar. Stir. Boil, uncovered, until thick, stirring as necessary. Pour into hot scalded jars [p. 28], leaving 1/2 inch (1 cm) headroom, and seal at once with snap lids and screw bands. Process in a boiling-water bath [p. 26] for 15 minutes.

Elderberry Juice I

ADD SOME RHUBARB JUICE [P. 44] TO THIS— A GREAT BREAKFAST DRINK. WHEN SERVING, DILUTE WITH WATER TO TASTE. USE DEAD-RIPE ELDERBERRIES.

Elderberry clusters

Lemon or sumac juice [p. 181]

Sugar

In a large preserving pot, cover elderberry clusters with water; remove most of the stalks which is easier after the berries are frozen. Simmer, covered, until soft and mushy. Pound fruit with a wooden mallet or large spoon to make sure all juice is cooked out of berries. Strain mixture through a jelly bag [p. 28] and let drip for several hours or overnight.

Measure juice. Heat, covered, to almost boiling. Add 1/2 cup (125 mL) sugar to each qt (L) juice, stirring until dissolved. Add lemon or sumac juice to taste. Bring mixture to a boil, reduce heat, and simmer, uncovered, for 5 to 10 minutes

Remove juice from heat. Pour into hot scalded jars [p. 28] leaving 1/2 inch (1 cm) headroom, and seal at once with snap lids and screw bands. Process in a boiling-water bath [p. 26] or steam canner for 15 minutes.

Elderberry Juice II

THIS IS A SIMPLE RECIPE: NO PRELIMINARY COOKING AND MASHING. USE DEAD-RIPE ELDERBERRIES, AND SERVE DILUTED WITH WATER TO TASTE.

Makes about 2 qt (2 L)

4 qt elderberries without stems (4 L)

Vinegar

Sugar

In a large preserving pot, cover elderberries with vinegar and let stand, covered, for 24 hours. Strain through a jelly bag [p. 28] and let drip until berries are dry.

Measure juice. Bring to a boil, covered, and stir in 2 cups (500 mL) sugar to each qt (L) juice. Simmer, covered, or with lid tilted, for 20 minutes, stirring as necessary.

Remove juice from heat. Pour into hot scalded jars [p. 28], leaving 1/2 inch (1 cm) headroom, and seal at once with snap lids and screw bands. Process in a boiling-water bath [p. 26] or steam canner for 15 minutes.

Elderberry Cordial

THIS MAKES A NICE AFTER-DINNER DRINK, AS WELL AS A TASTY BASE FOR A HOT TODDY IF YOU HAVE A COLD. ELDERBERRY JUICES AND DRINKS HAVE LONG BEEN ASSOCIATED WITH SOOTHING THE SYMPTOMS OF COLDS AND CONGESTION. USE DEAD-RIPE ELDERBERRIES.

Makes about 3 qt (3 L)

8 qt elderberries without stems (3 L)
8 tsp whole allspice (40 mL)
1 cinnamon stick
2 qt water (2 L)
Sugar
2 tsp whole cloves (10 mL)
Brandy

In a large preserving pot, combine elderberries, water, cloves, allspice, and cinnamon. Boil, covered, until berries are soft. Strain mixture. Measure juice and stir in 1 1/2 cups (375 mL) sugar to each qt (L) juice. Simmer, uncovered, until mixture begins to thicken, about 30 minutes.

Remove syrup from heat and let cool. Measure syrup and stir in 1 cup (250 mL) brandy to each qt (L) syrup. Pour into bottles and seal with screw caps. Store in a cool, dry cupboard.

Note: To make *hot toddies,* add hot water to desired amount of cordial.

Elderberry Wine

The following proportions make a medium-dry red wine; increase or decrease the amount of sugar for a sweeter or drier wine. Use clean dead-ripe elderberries.

3 1/2 lb elderberries (1.75 kg)
1 Tbsp wine or baking yeast (15 mL)
1 lemon, sliced
7 pt water (3.5 L)
Sugar

In a large preserving pot, combine elderberries, lemon, and water. Simmer, covered, until fruit is soft, mashing to expel juice. Strain mixture through a jelly bag [p. 28] and let drip overnight. Squeeze bag to extract trapped liquid. Simmer pulp, covered, and strain again.

Dissolve yeast in a little warm water. Combine and measure liquid from extractions. Place in a large crock or plastic bucket and stir in 2 lb (1 kg) sugar to each gallon (4 L) juice. Add yeast and stir mixture again. Cover container with a plastic bag and tie bag. Let mixture ferment at 70° to 75°F (20° to 25°C) until obvious bubbling ceases.

Siphon contents into glass jugs, using cotton plugs as stoppers. Store wine at 60° to 65°F (15° to 18°C), away from direct sunlight. When wine stops bubbling completely (in about 1 month), resiphon into permanent bottles. Seal and store in a cool, dark, dry place. If using corks, store bottles lying down.

Dried Elderberries

Before using dried elderberries, steep them in hot water. Save the juice and use it in cooking or baking. Add some dried berries to winter apple pies for more flavor.

Harvest ripest clusters of elderberries and gently pull berries from their stems. Place on cookie sheets or large flat pans. Set them in sun or in a just-warm oven to dry. Stir them often and shake pan to prevent berries from sticking. Dry berries until free of liquid. To test, squeeze one.

Freezing Elderberries

Store elderberries, with or without stems, in a freezer bag or freezer container, for future use. No sugar is needed. Frozen elderberries are much easier to de-stem than fresh elderberries.

Elderflower Pancakes

ALL YOUR DELICIOUS SASSES WILL TASTE TERRIFIC ON THESE LIGHT ELDERFLOWER PANCAKES.

Serves 2

1/2 cup elderflorets (125 mL)
1 Tbsp cornmeal (15 mL)
1/2 cup unbleached all-purpose flour (125 mL)
1 egg
2 Tbsp melted butter, shortening, or lard (25 mL)
1/2 tsp baking soda (2 mL)
2 Tbsp sugar (25 mL)
1/2 to 1 cup buttermilk (125 to 250 mL)
1/2 tsp salt (2 mL)

Cut clusters of elderflowers and shake off florets. Set florets aside. Sift together flour, baking soda, sugar, salt, and cornmeal.

In a bowl, beat egg well and stir in melted butter and 1/2 cup (125 mL) buttermilk, mixing only until flour is blended in; do not overstir. Stir in elderflorets and more buttermilk until batter reaches desired consistency.

Ladle pancakes onto a hot greased griddle and cook until nicely browned.

Note: Lighten and flavor any bread, roll, or muffin recipe with elderflowers by substituting 1 cup (250 mL) florets for 1 cup (250 mL) flour.

Variation: To make *buttermilk pancakes,* omit florets and increase amount of flour to 1 cup (250 mL). Stir in additional buttermilk until batter reaches consistency of muffin dough or thinner, depending on how you like your pancakes. Great with all fruit toppings.

Elderflowers

Elderflower-Peppermint Tea

THIS IS A SOOTHING DRINK FOR RELIEF FROM COLD SYMPTOMS—OR IT'S JUST NICE TO HAVE ON A WINTER AFTERNOON. THE FOLLOWING PROPORTIONS ARE FOR DRIED FLOWERS AND MINT; INCREASE THE AMOUNTS IF USING FRESH BLOSSOMS AND LEAVES.

Makes 1 cup (250 mL)

1 heaping tsp elderflower blossoms (5 mL)
1 cup boiling water (250 mL)
1 heaping tsp dried peppermint leaves (5 mL)

Put elderflower blossoms and mint leaves in a tea egg. Place egg in a teacup. Add boiling water, cover, and let steep for a few minutes. Sweeten to taste with honey if desired.

Elderflower Fritters

Serve this dessert on a summer evening.

Serves 2

Elderflowers with stems

Batter:

Brandy
2 egg yolks
1 cinnamon stick (optional)
2/3 cup milk (150 mL)
1 cup flour (250 mL)
Orange juice
1 Tbsp sugar (15 mL)
Icing sugar
Dash salt

On the morning of a sunny day, cut clusters of fully opened elderflowers, leaving about a 6-inch (15-cm) stem. Refrigerate in a plastic bag until 1 hour before cooking.

In a bowl, combine brandy and cinnamon stick. Add and submerge flower heads. Let stand for 1 hour.

Meanwhile, in a separate bowl, make batter by mixing together egg yolks, milk, flour, salt, and sugar.

Drain flower heads and shake dry. Holding each cluster by its stem, dip flowers in batter. Fry them immediately in 2 inches (5 cm) hot fat in a cast-iron frying pan. (Fry up to 3 clusters at once.) Remove when lightly browned, drain on paper, and sprinkle with a little icing sugar and a bit of orange juice. Serve at once.

Elderberry Pie Deluxe

1 cup or less sugar (250 mL or less)
2 cups ripe elderberries (500 mL)
2 eggs, separated
2 Tbsp cornstarch (25 mL)
1 cup sour cream (250 mL)
Baked pie shell [p. 46]

In a bowl, mix together sugar and egg yolks. Stir in sour cream until well blended. In a separate bowl, combine elderberries and cornstarch; fold into sugar mixture.

In a saucepan, cook berry mixture over low heat until thick, stirring often. Pour into a baked 9-inch (23-cm) pie shell.

In a bowl, beat egg whites until stiff and spread over pie filling. Bake pie in a 350°F (180°C) oven until meringue is lightly browned.

Elderberry Pie

Pastry [p. 46]
1 Tbsp lemon juice or vinegar (15 mL)
3 cups ripe elderberries (750 mL)
1 cup or less sugar (250 mL or less)
Pinch salt
2 Tbsp flour (25 mL)

Line a 9-inch (23-cm) pie plate with pastry and fill with elderberries. In a bowl, mix together remaining ingredients; pour over berries. Cover pie with a top crust and prick a few times with a fork. Bake in a 350°F (180°C) oven for about 40 minutes or until crust is browned and berries are bubbling.

Note: To make with dried elderberries [p. 126], pour boiling water over 3 cups (750 mL) or more dried berries. Let steep until soft, drain, and proceed as above.

To make with elderberry preserves [p. 122], drain preserves and measure 2 1/2 to 3 cups (625 to 750 mL) elderberries. Omit lemon or vinegar and proceed. If using elderberry preserves that do not contain vinegar, do not omit lemon or vinegar.

Elderberry-Custard Pie

SERVE PIECES OF THIS ELEGANT PIE WITH WHIPPED CREAM.

4 Tbsp flour (75 mL)
1 cup elderberry juice [p. 124] (250 mL)
1 cup or less sugar (250 mL or less)
1/4 tsp salt (2 mL)
1 egg, separated
1 cup milk (250 mL)
Unbaked pie shell [p. 46]

In a bowl, combine flour, sugar, and salt. Stir in enough milk to make a paste.

In a saucepan, bring elderberry juice to a boil. Stir paste into hot juice. Simmer, stirring often to prevent lumps. Remove from heat and stir in remaining milk to cool mixture. Stir in egg yolk.

Beat egg white in a bowl until stiff; fold into juice mixture. Pour filling into an unbaked 9-inch (23-cm) pie shell and bake in a 350°F (180°C) oven for about 30 minutes.

Citron Melon

Until quite recently, I thought that the citron I grew in the garden was the same as the kind that was used to make candied citron. Those tiny pale-green translucent squares, sticky and sweet, are indispensable for fruitcake making. And every year, in the late fall, they turn up on food-store shelves in stacks of shallow plastic containers next to glacé cherries and candied pineapple.

I know now, thanks to *Wyman's Gardening Encyclopedia* and my trusty *Ball Blue Book* on preserving (1982), that there are two kinds of citron. One citron, the kind used for making those candied squares, grows on a tree and is called *Citrus medica.* The fruit is 6 to 10 inches (15 to 25 cm) long and 4 to 6 inches (10 to 15 cm) wide. The other citron, my citron, is a member of the watermelon family and is called *Citrullus lanatus* var. *citroides,* referred to as "the preserving melon" or "citron melon." Native to Africa, it was grown in America before 1863. Like other melons, it grows on a vine. When mature, these citrons are round, striped light and dark green, and weigh 5 to 8 lb (2.5 to 4 kg). Both tree and vine citron have thick rinds suitable for making the candied fruit, and in addition, the old-fashioned preserving melon has been used for hundreds of years as an easily grown, reliable source for making pickles, marmalade, and preserves, items that had a place on the well-stocked shelves of the winter larder years ago.

Although I might be able to grow *Citrus medica* if I lived in southern Florida or in Texas, I know that with a little care I can always grow the preserving melon, even in my northern garden. Now regarded as an heirloom, seeds are hard to come by (see Appendix). There is little difference between the two varieties that may be available, green- or red-seeded. Either packet of seeds will bring a large crop of handsome striped fruit. If you enjoy the challenge of making things, you will get a kick out of making those little squares. If you can't stand fruitcake (try my recipe first before you make up your mind), make pickles, preserves, or marmalade. Friends will be glad to take some of the fruit off your hands, too, as citrons make marvelous centerpieces and fall decorations. With their tough outer rind, they keep for many months in a cool, sunny spot protected from freezing temperatures, and they are a handsome addition to the usual gourds, pumpkins, and Indian corn.

Planting

If you live in the northeast, there is a trick to growing citron—and all melons, for that matter. First, you must provide the plants with a long growing season, about 95 days. Second, you must provide them with more heat than is normally available during a typical summer. Both these conditions can be easily met by raising seedlings and then planting them out with a plastic mulch. Such a mulch absorbs and retains a great deal of heat even if there is little sun available.

To begin with, find suitable containers in which to grow the seedlings: old strawberry boxes, large-sized jiffy pots, or any recycled container of similar size that will break down when planted in soil. But line the strawberry boxes with moss or other material first, to keep the dirt from spilling out through the openings, and choose the sod from an area that has well-drained soil. The point is to raise seedlings in a container that is large enough to accommodate the growing roots and that can be planted intact without disturbing the roots.

About a month before your last-expected frost, in the spring, fill suitable containers—six will suffice unless you have a market for the fruit—with any rich well-drained friable soil that has been lightened with a little vermiculite. Tamp the soil, leaving watering space, water the containers, and set them in a cold frame, greenhouse, or on a sunny windowsill until the soil has warmed. Seventy-five to eighty degrees Fahrenheit (25° to 27°C) will give the best germination.

To plant, sow about 5 to 6 seeds in each container. Push the seeds gently into the soil until they are covered; if using sod, cover the seeds with soil. Keep the soil moist and warm, two imperatives for germinating citron seeds, as well as for growing seedlings, if you are using a cold frame, cover it with a heavy blanket on cool nights. When the seedlings are established, thin them to 2 to 3 per container. (Cut the extras with scissors.)

When transplanting the seedlings, it's best to give them their own patch so that they don't eventually interfere with other garden crops—citrons like to sprawl. Choose an area at one side of the garden, an area enriched, perhaps, with well-rotted compost. Citrons prefer light, sandy loam, but any garden soil will do if it is fairly rich and well drained. With a hoe, mark holes about 8 ft (2.5 m) apart, making little hills to provide good drainage. On a cloudy, windless, warm day, when all danger of frost has passed, set each well-watered container in its hill, firmly tamping the dirt around the stems of the seedlings. If you have used strawberry baskets, remove them by cutting down each side with scissors and slide the block of soil and roots gently into place.

As soon as the citrons are planted, they should be mulched. To mulch, take a piece of plastic (black is good because it absorbs heat, but any will suffice) about 18 inches x 30 inches (45 cm x 75 cm). Cut a slit in the middle and set the whole piece over the plant. Carefully lift the leaves through the slit and over the sides of the plastic so that the plant can grow on top while the roots remain underneath, heated by their little greenhouse. Heap dirt or rocks—rocks also retain heat—along the sides of the plastic to prevent blowing. In a dry spell, water the plants every day until they are well established.

Cultivating

During the early stages of growth, the area surrounding the young plants will probably need to be cultivated with a hoe. Weeds growing under the mulch, if there are any, will usually die from overheating. Aside from pulling large weeds that interfere with the spreading vines, there is little else to do. If you have raised healthy seedlings, the citron plants should be vigorous enough to shade out weeds, and the plastic mulch will help, too.

Harvesting

Citrons do not take kindly to cold, freezing temperatures, so harvest them all before the first frost. Leave about 2 inches (5 cm) of stem for a handle. One of the nicest things about harvesting citron, in addition to discovering more fruits under the canopy of leaves, is knowing that you needn't do anything with them for months, until all your other harvesting and processing work is done. Besides, you should leave citrons to ripen for a few months in a cool, sunny room. Be sure they are prominently displayed because everyone who sees them will admire them and want to know what they are.

Preserving, Canning, And Cooking

The citron is made up of an outer rind (not counting the thick skin) and an inner section of seeds. The outer rind is larger by far, and it is with this "meat" that you make candied citron, pickles, preserves, or marmalade. Citron is only edible when it is preserved, and even then it is rather bland and sweet. Nonetheless, its texture makes products interesting, and I include one recipe that calls for fresh rind. Review A Short Course in Fruit Preserving [p. 4] before preserving.

Citron Cake

THIS IS AN OLD RECIPE THAT USES FRESH CITRON.

1/4 lb butter (125 g)
1 1/2 tsp baking powder (7 mL)
1 cup sugar (250 mL)
1 Tbsp brandy (15 mL)
3 eggs, separated
1 cup citron rind, sliced thin and chopped (250 mL)
1/2 cup milk (125 mL)
1 cup flour (250 mL)

In a bowl, cream butter, add sugar, and beat well. Gradually add egg yolks and milk, mixing and beating thoroughly. Sift together flour and baking powder; add to sugar-egg mixture, beating well.

In a separate bowl, beat egg whites until stiff; fold into batter. Fold in brandy and citron. Pour batter into a greased 9-inch (22 cm) tube pan and bake in a 350°F (180°C) oven for about 1 hour or until knife or cake tester inserted near center comes out clean.

Citron Marmalade

This is similar in taste to orange or citrus-fruit marmalade, but the citron cuts the usual bitterness.

Makes about 5 pt (2.5 L)

3 lb citron (1.5 kg)
4 lb sugar (2 kg)
3 lb oranges and lemons, mixed (1.5 kg)

Cut citron into quarters, remove seeds, and peel outer skin. Slice rind very thin and cut into small pieces.

Thinly slice oranges and lemons and cut into small pieces, removing seeds. In a large stainless-steel pot, combine fruit and sugar. Cover and let stand overnight.

Bring to a boil, uncover, reduce heat, and simmer until thick, stirring as necessary.

Remove marmalade from heat and let subside. Stir. Fill hot scalded jars [p. 28] to 1/4 inch (5 mm) from the top and seal at once with snap lids and screw bands. Process in a boiling-water bath [p. 26] or steam canner for 10 minutes.

Candied Citron

Although made primarily for fruitcake, candied citron can be included in many cake and cookie recipes.

Makes about 1 lb (500 g)

2 medium-sized citrons
2 cups water (500 mL)
4 cups sugar (1 L)
2 Tbsp corn syrup (25 mL)

Cut citrons into quarters and remove seeds but do not peel. Place in a large preserving pot and add water. Cover and simmer until tender. Drain and cool.

Slice off outer skin and cut fruit into desired shapes, usually 1/4-inch (5-mm) squares. Drain overnight in a colander.

In a saucepan, combine sugar and 2 cups (500 mL) water and bring to a boil. Boil syrup until it reaches softball stage. Remove from heat and stir in citron squares. Let stand in syrup overnight.

Drain and roll squares in sugar. Place on a cookie sheet and dry slowly in a 250°F (120°C) oven. Turn off heat and let citron remain in oven until squares are quite firm.

Variation: To make *candied orange peel* or *candied lemon peel,* substitute peel of 2 dozen medium-sized oranges or lemons for citron.

Citron Pickles

YOU CAN SUBSTITUTE PREPARED CITRON CHUNKS FOR OVERRIPE CUCUMBER IN ANY PICKLE RECIPE.

Makes about 4 pt (2 L)

4 lb citron rind (2 kg)
1/2 oz cinnamon sticks (15 g)
Water
1 Tbsp whole cloves (15 mL)
1 Tbsp whole allspice (15 mL)
1 pt cider vinegar (500 mL)
2 lemons, sliced thin
3 cups brown sugar (750 mL)
Salt

Cut citrons into quarters, scoop out seedy middle, and peel tough outer skin. Cut remaining fruit, or rind, into small chunks about 1 inch (2.5 cm) square or desired size. Weigh fruit.

In a large preserving pot, combine water and salt, using 3 Tbsp (50 mL) salt to each qt (L) water. Use enough water to cover chopped rind. Place 4 lb (2 kg) rind in saltwater, cover, and let soak overnight.

Drain rind and cover with fresh boiling water. Simmer, covered, or with lid tilted, until citron is tender, checking occasionally to make sure water hasn't boiled away. Drain again.

In a separate pot, combine vinegar and sugar and bring to a boil. Tie up spices in a cheesecloth bag; add to vinegar-sugar mixture. Add citron and sliced lemons. Stirring occasionally, simmer whole mixture, uncovered, until fruit is clear.

Remove spice bag and ladle mixture into hot scalded jars [p. 28], leaving 1/2 inch (5 mm) headspace and seal at once with snap lids and screw bands. Process in a boiling-water bath [p. 27] or steam canner for 10 minutes.

Citron Preserves

SERVE THESE PRESERVES WITH CHOCOLATE ICE CREAM, OR DRAIN AND USE THEM IN FRUITCAKE AS A SUBSTITUTE FOR CANDIED CITRON.

Makes about 3 pt (1.5 L)

3 lb citron (1.5 kg)
Juice of 1 lemon
2 lb sugar (2 kg)

Cut citron into quarters, remove seeds, and peel outer skin. Slice rind very thin and cut into small pieces. Place in a large preserving pot. Add sugar, mix thoroughly, cover, and let stand overnight.

Bring mixture to a boil and simmer, uncovered, until citron is transparent. Add lemon juice and cook for a few more minutes.

Remove preserves from heat. Ladle into hot scalded jars [p. 28], leaving 1/2 inch (5 mm) headroom, and seal at once with snap lids and screw bands. Process in a boiling-water bath [p. 26] or steam canner for 15 minutes.

Nova Scotia Fruitcake

Makes 2

4 oz candied citron, coarsely chopped [p. 135] (125 g)
2 oz candied lemon peel, coarsely chopped [p. 135] (50 g)
2 oz candied orange peel, coarsely chopped [p. 135] (50 g)
1/2 lb candied cherries, halved (250 g)
1 lb candied pineapple, shredded (500 g)
1 lb golden raisins (500 g)
1/2 lb seeded raisins (250 g)
4 oz dried black currants [p. 108] (125 g)
1/2 cup dark rum, cognac, or sherry (125 mL)
4 oz almonds, coarsely chopped (125 g)
4 oz walnuts, coarsely chopped (125 g)
4 oz pecans, coarsely chopped (125 g)
2 cups unbleached all-purpose flour, sifted (500 mL)
1/2 tsp mace (2 mL)
1/2 tsp cinnamon (2 mL)
1/2 tsp baking powder (2 mL)
1 tsp almond extract (5 mL)
1 Tbsp milk (15 mL)
1/2 cup butter (125 mL)
1 cup granulated sugar(250 mL)
1 packed cup brown sugar (250 mL)
5 eggs
Rum, cognac, or sherry

In a large bowl, mix together candied citron, lemon peel, orange peel, cherries, pineapple, golden raisins, seeded raisins, and dried black currants. Stir in 1/2 cup (125 mL) rum to evenly coat ingredients. Cover and let stand overnight.

Combine fruits, almonds, walnuts, pecans, and 1/2 cup (125 mL) flour. Sift together remaining flour, mace, cinnamon, and baking powder. Set aside.

In a small bowl, stir almond extract into milk. In a large bowl, cream butter, add granulated and brown sugars and eggs, mixing well. Stir in milk mixture and then sifted dry ingredients. Beat well. Pour batter over fruit-nut mixture and mix well.

Grease two 9-inch (3-L) tube pans. Line each with greased wax paper, even tube in middle. Pack pans with batter, pressing batter firmly all around. Place a pan of hot water in bottom of oven. Bake cakes in a 275°F (140°C) oven for about 3 1/2 hours or less, until a sharp knife or cake tester inserted near center comes out clean. *Do not overbake.*

Remove cakes from oven and let stand for 30 minutes. Turn out onto a cake rack, peel off paper, and let cakes cool. Wrap in rum-, cognac-, or sherry-soaked cheesecloth and place in deep tins lined with thick layers of wax paper, making sure each tin has a tight lid. As cloths dry out, dribble more liquor over them. This should probably be done twice over the space of 2 months. Let age for at least 4 months.

An Assortment of Basics

There are several more simple ways to preserve fruit or prepare it for the table. The small fruits are quite versatile and can be used interchangeably in any of the following basic recipes. Mix and match any way you like—all the recipes are guaranteed to please those lucky enough to taste the results.

Basic Butters, Cheeses, Pastes

Butters, cheeses, and pastes were ways to preserve a bountiful harvest of fruits, especially apples, peaches, plums, and quinces, but almost any fruit can be used. Basically, the fruit is reduced by cooking it up, skins, cores, or pits, with spices, if desired, tied up in cheesecloth. When the fruit is soft it is put through a food mill to remove skins and seeds (apples, quince) or pits (plums) to produce a smooth purée. Sugar is added and the mixture is cooked slowly, stirred often to prevent scorching, until the desired consistency: Butter is spreadable and should mound on a spoon; cheeses and pastes are drier and can be cut into slices, squares, or different shapes.

For butters, add 1/2 to 1 cup (125 to 250 mL) sugar for 1 cup (250 mL) of purée, or according to taste. When the mixture is thick and mounds on a spoon without sliding off it is done; don't overcook. Pour or spoon into hot scalded canning jars or jelly jars [p. 6], leaving 1/4 inch (5 mm) headroom. Process jars in a boiling-water bath [p. 4] or steam canner for 10 minutes.

For cheeses and pastes, add sugar by weight of the purée; for a less sweet product, add sugar by volume of the purée. Store in refrigerator for up to 3 months, or freeze.

Basic Brandied Fruit

Brandied fruits are, to put it mildly, a sensation when served over pancakes with a dab of sour cream and a bit of red currant sass. You needn't brandy much fruit—a little goes a long way, and once it's preserved, the mixture can be poured into jars, sealed, processed, and stored until the day you want to dish up a deluxe breakfast. Use high-quality firm ripe fruit, and never add more than 2 qt (2 L) at a time. Besides strawberries and raspberries, consider cherries, peaches (peeled and sliced), apricots, pineapple, bananas, orange slices, and blueberries.

Brandy
Sugar
Fruit

Put 1 qt (1 L) brandy in a 2-gallon (8-L) crock or container that has a tight-fitting lid. Add fruit in season. Stir in 2 cups (500 mL) sugar to each qt (L) fruit. Stir well after each addition and keep container covered. After 2 months, ladle brandied fruit into hot scalded jars [p. 28], leaving 1/2 inch (1 cm) headspace, and seal at once. Process in a boiling-water bath [p. 26] or steam canner for 15 minutes.

Basic Fruit Shrub

A shrub is an old, reliable way to preserve fresh-fruit flavor. It is a concentrated liquid used for making summer drinks, alcoholic or nonalcoholic. Turn any dead-ripe or overripe fruit into shrubs by steeping it in cider vinegar and heating the resulting liquid with sugar. To serve, add about 4 parts water to 1 part shrub, adding brandy to taste if desired.

Fruit
Sugar
Cider vinegar

In a large preserving pot, cover fruit with cider vinegar. Cover and let stand for 24 hours.

Strain and measure juice. For each pt (500 mL) juice, add 1 pt (500 mL) sugar. Boil together, uncovered, for 10 minutes.

Skim mixture. Pour into hot scalded jars [p. 28], leaving 1/4 inch (5 mm) headroom, and seal at once with snap lids and screw bands. Process in a boiling water bath [p. 26] or steam canner for 10 minutes.

Basic Fruit Soup

There are many versions of fruit soups. Some are served hot, some cold. Some are served as appetizers, others as desserts. This recipe came from a Mennonite friend who lives in Central America. The soup is served cold, and the fruit is only cut up, not puréed, as in most recipes. Soup made from cooked, puréed fruit is usually heated, thickened with cornstarch, and then thinned with milk or cream.

Serves 5 to 6

2 cups cut-up fruit (500 mL)
1 heaping Tbsp flour or cornstarch (15 mL)
2 cups water (500 mL)
1 cup sugar (250 mL)
1 Tbsp sugar (15 mL)
1 qt creamy milk (1 L)

In a pot, combine fruit, water, and 1 cup (500 mL) sugar. Simmer, covered, for 10 minutes.

In a large bowl, make a paste out of flour or cornstarch, 1 Tbsp (15 mL) sugar, and a little milk. Gradually stir in all milk. Stir milk mixture into fruit. Chill thoroughly.

Basic Berry Ice

BERRY ICES ARE JUST FROZEN SYRUPS—CHILDREN LIKE THEM AS POPSICLES. USE SMALL FRUITS SUCH AS STRAWBERRIES, RASPBERRIES, AND RED CURRANTS.

Serves 5 to 6

4 to 6 cups berries (1 to 1.5 L)
4 cups water (1 L)
1 1/2 cups sugar (375 mL)

Prepare berry juice. Mash and strain ripe or overripe berries. Measure 2 cups (500 mL) juice. Set aside. (Or use juice left over from jelly making.)

In a large pot, combine sugar and water. Bring mixture to a boil, stirring to dissolve sugar. Remove from heat and stir in berry juice. Pour mixture into small molds or cups and freeze. To remove ice when serving, plunge molds into cold water.

Note: You can substitute 3/4 to 1 cup (175 to 250 mL) honey for the sugar.

To make berry ice from presweetened canned juice or juice drained from preserves, omit sugar.

To make *red currant-raspberry ice,* use 1 1/3 cups (325 mL) red currant juice and 2/3 cup (150 mL) raspberry juice.

To make popsicles, insert popsicle sticks in each mold when mixture begins to freeze. Then continue freezing.

Basic Fruit Ice Cream

We use a 6-qt (6-L) White Mountain Ice Cream Maker for this. Use any ripe fruit you want and sweet cream that is fresh and not too thick. To increase fruit flavor, just decrease cream and increase fruit purée.

Makes 4 qt (4 L)
3 qt sweet cream (3 L)
2 qt fruit (2 L)
3 cups sugar (750 mL)

Chill canister of ice-cream maker. In a pot, heat 1 qt (1 L) cream slowly. Stir in sugar and continue heating and stirring until it is dissolved in cream. Remove cream from heat and chill.

Meanwhile, purée fruit. Mash, crush, grind, or put it through a food mill or blender, depending on toughness and desired consistency. Press seedy fruits such as raspberries through a strainer if desired. Measure 1 qt (1 L) purée. Sprinkle purée with sugar to taste, stir, and let stand, covered, at room temperature until ready to use.

Pour chilled cream into chilled canister. Stir in remaining cream. Set canister in ice-cream-maker tub and pack rock salt and ice around it, using 1 part salt to 5 parts ice. Cover and churn until mixture is thick and handle starts to resist turning (about 700 turns).

Carefully remove lid of canister and pour in fruit, stirring it in carefully with a long-handled wooden spoon. Re-cover and churn until handle is difficult to turn (200 to 300 turns). Remove dasher and re-cover canister. Pack chipped ice all around canister where necessary, cover ice cream maker with burlap, and set in a cool place.

Note: You can substitute 2 to 2 1/2 cups (500 to 625 mL) honey for the sugar.

Before making *black currant ice cream,* stew black currants in a little water, adding sugar to taste. Put mixture through a food mill and add to nearly frozen ice cream, as above.

Variation: To make *vanilla ice cream* to go with fruit sauces, omit fruit purée and use 4 qt (4 L) cream and 4 tsp (20 mL) vanilla. Heat 1 qt (1 L) cream, stir in sugar and vanilla, chill, and add to chilled canister with 3 qt (3 L) cream.

Several years ago, friends Sue and Henry Bass gave me a nifty electric ice cream maker so I could experiment with making small amounts of specialty ice cream, including fruit sherbert, sorbet/ices, and frozen fruit yogurt. Directions may vary according to the machine you use. The ones below are based on my 1990s Oster Ice Cream/Frozen Yogurt Maker which produces no more than 1 1/2 quarts (1.5 L) finished product and uses ice cubes and table salt for freezing. You will need approximately 2 cups table salt (500 mL) and 6 trays of small ice cubes, or 9 cups (2.12 L). Feel free to alter the recipes to achieve the taste you prefer (fruitier or sweeter), but be sure to confine yourself to the total liquid amount which is based on the capacity of the machine.

Strawberry Ice Cream

Basic Fruit Sherbert

SHERBERTS, AS DISTINCT FROM ICE CREAM, USE MILK AS THE BASE. INCREASE FRUIT JUICE AND DECREASE MILK FOR A FRUITIER FLAVOR. A LOT WILL DEPEND ON THE FRUIT JUICE YOU USE.

Makes about 1 1/2 quarts (1.5 L)

cups milk (750 mL)
2 cups unsweetened fruit juice (500 mL)
1 cup sugar (250 mL)

Combine ingredients in canister, stirring well. Cover with freezing cover, and chill for faster freezing. When ready to begin freezing, turn on the machine, set canister in ice bucket, pour in water and layer ice and salt as directed. Remove freezing cover, insert paddle, and put mixing cover in place, adding more water according to directions. Turn on machine and add more salt and ice as directed when ice begins to melt. Continue freezing until sherbert is the consistency you want. This should take about 20-25 minutes, or less in my experience. Remove canister, stir to blend if necessary, store in freezer for an hour or more, then you may remove sherbert to a plastic freezer container and return to freezer.

Strawberry Gelatin

Basic Fruit Gelatin

There are many ways to get the juice for gelatin: canned juices, juice drained from preserves, or cooked-and-strained fresh fruit. All sorts of combinations are possible, too. When serving gelatin, whipped cream would not be amiss.

Serves 5 to 6

2 envelopes gelatin
3 cups presweetened juice (750 mL)
1 cup cold water (250 mL)

In a saucepan, sprinkle gelatin over cold water. Place over low heat and stir constantly until gelatin dissolves or no granules are visible.

Remove from heat and stir in juice. Pour gelatin into a Pyrex baking dish or bread pan and chill for several hours or until firm. If adding cut-up fresh fruit—sliced bananas, oranges, or strawberries—fold into gelatin when it begins to jell. Chill until firm.

Note: To make with fresh fruit, cook desired fruit with a little water, mashing to extract as much juice as possible. When fruit is well heated and juicy, strain and measure 3 cups (750 mL) juice; stir in 1/2 cup (125 mL) sugar and proceed as above.

Basic Frozen Fruit Yogurt

Makes about 1 1/2 quarts (1.5 L)

1 cup fruit, fresh or frozen (250 mL)
1 cup sugar (250 mL)
1 quart plain yogurt (1 L)

Place fruit and sugar in a blender and process at medium speed until smooth. Pour into canister and combine with yogurt, stirring well. Cover with freezing cover, and chill for faster freezing. When ready to begin freezing, turn on the machine, set canister in ice bucket, pour in water and layer ice and salt as directed. Remove freezing cover, insert paddle, and put mixing cover in place, adding more water according to directions. Turn on machine and add more salt and ice as directed when ice begins to melt. Continue freezing until frozen yogurt is the consistency you want. This should take about 12-20 minutes. Remove canister, stir to blend if necessary, store in freezer for an hour or more, then you may remove frozen yogurt to a plastic freezer container and return to freezer.

Basic Fruit Sorbet/Ice

Makes about 1 quart (1 L)

1 cup water (250 mL)
2 cups unsweetened fruit juice (500 mL)
2 cups sugar (500 mL)

Sorbets and ices are synonymous; both use water, instead of cream or milk, as the base. Combine ingredients in canister, stirring well. Cover with freezing cover, and chill for faster freezing. When ready to begin freezing, turn on the machine, set canister in ice bucket, pour in water and layer ice and salt as directed. Remove freezing cover, insert paddle, and put mixing cover in place, adding more water according to directions. Turn on machine and add more salt and ice as directed when ice begins to melt. Continue freezing until sorbet/ice is the consistency you want. This should take about 12-20 minutes, or less in my experience. Remove canister, stir to blend if necessary, store in freezer for an hour or more, then you may remove sorbet/ice to a plastic freezer container and return to freezer.

Tree Fruits and Wild Fruits

There are, of course, many more fruits that you can grow and harvest if climate, soil, and space allow. Fruit trees that require a lot of sun, deep soil, careful pruning and, usually, cross-pollination add another dimension to the fruit garden. But even if you cannot grow them, some tree fruits, such as apples, are there for the picking, anyway, or are available from local orchards.

Fruits from the wild—blackberries, blueberries, cranberries—can be harvested and processed to complement the produce from a cultivated garden. It is exciting and satisfying to become acquainted with all the useful vegetation that survives from year to year without being tended.

Still other fruits, particularly pears and peaches, are often available in large quantities on the market. *The thing to remember is that no matter how you get your fruit, give some thought to its handling.* Decide how to take advantage fully of what a fruit has to offer. Turn high-pectin fruits into jams and jellies, overripe fruits into wines and juices, odds and ends of fruits into leathers. And, most important, always use the technology most suited to the task, the least damaging to the environment and, ultimately, the most satisfying. With a few simple hand tools, some ordinary kitchen equipment, and a basic knowledge of preserving, you can put the heart and soul back into the fruit harvest. Review Short Course [p. 4] before preserving.

Tree Fruits

If you decide to include tree fruits in your garden, study the varieties, and the methods of cultivation first. Take a look at dwarf and semi-dwarf trees, too—they take up less space than standard-sized varieties. Some dwarf types can even be grown in tubs.

Apples

The number of apple recipes here attests to the hardiness of apples in northern climates. In mid-June, the ground around our trees is thickly covered with white blossoms. On our farm, by fall, our porch was full of buckets of apples to turn into sundry products, to eat, to feed to livestock, or to give to friends and neighbors.

It has been said that the function of the apple tree is to "bottle sunshine." There are more kinds of apples to choose from now than there have been for some time, among both heirlooms and newer introductions. Standard types grow from 18 to 25 ft tall (5.5 to 7.6 m) and bear in 3 to 6 years. The semi-dwarf types may grow from 6 to 12 ft tall (1.8 to 3.7 m) and bear in their third or fourth year, but they don't last as long as standards. Bear in mind that you need two different varieties for proper pollination. Even if you don't grow your own, you can find many abandoned productive apple trees in the countryside. Many old varieties are still recognizable, and they are useful for more than cider making; for example, Wolf River for dried apples and Duchess for applesauce. Ultimately, you need not know their names, just their qualities. Whether in your backyard or in some deserted orchard, look for apples that lend themselves to the following recipes. And don't forget to ask for permission before you pick. Failing that, local orchards and farm stands are your best bet for buying better quality apples in quantity for preserving.

Apple Butter III

We can call this a jam to distinguish it from the other spiced-and-sugared apple butters. Sweet apples and fresh sweet cider are a must for this recipe. This butter is delightful on English muffins.

Apple cider
Apples

In a large preserving pot, boil fresh cider, uncovered, until reduced by half. Stir occasionally. Pare and quarter (no need to peel) enough sweet apples to fill up cider. Stirring frequently with a wooden spoon, boil slowly until mixture is consistency of marmalade. Remove butter from heat. Jar, seal, and process as for Apple Butter I.

Dried Apple Rings

THE DRIED APPLE INDUSTRY, DEVELOPED IN WESTERN NEW YORK, USED TO BE VERY IMPORTANT WHEN FRESH OR FROZEN APPLES WERE NOT WIDELY AVAILABLE. MANY EARLY APPLE PIE RECIPES, FOR INSTANCE, CALLED FOR USING DRIED APPLES. NOT ONLY WERE CONDITIONS FAVORABLE FOR GROWING APPLES IN WESTERN NEW YORK, BUT BY 1825, WITH THE ESTABLISHMENT OF THE ERIE CANAL, DRIED APPLES COULD BE SHIPPED ALL OVER THE WORLD. BY THE 1940S, HOWEVER, THE INDUSTRY DWINDLED, AS FRESH APPLES, NO LONGER A LUXURY, COULD BE SHIPPED ACROSS THE COUNTRY OR KEPT COLD IN THE HOME REFRIGERATOR. WE, LIKE THE PIONEERS OF OLD, SOUGHT ALTERNATIVE WAYS TO STORE OUR BOUNTIFUL APPLE HARVEST UNTIL THE NEXT GROWING SEASON. DRIED APPLE RINGS WERE THE ANSWER.

Peel and core fairly uniform large winter apples, reserving cores and peelings for jelly. Slice apple rings about 1/8 to 1/4 inch (3 to 5 mm) thick and hang them about 1/2 inch (1 cm) apart on clean sticks or dowels. Balance sticks across deep roasting pans and place pans wherever apple rings will be exposed to circulating dry air. Or suspend them above stove, where rings will receive some heat during cooking.

When rings feel dry and a little leathery or papery, not hard or crisp, and are pale amber in color, they are done. Store them in covered crocks or jars. They will keep almost indefinitely.

Variation: Use the cores and peelings to make *apple-peelings jelly,* the tastiest, fastest-setting jelly. Broken rings, of course, can be added to the pot. Just follow the recipe for apple jelly [p. 149], using 6 cups (1.5 L) cores and peelings and 4 cups (1 L) water.

Apple Jelly

Makes at least 2 pt (1 L)

5 lb apples (2.5 kg)
Sugar
5 cups cold water (1.25 L)

Cut up tart fresh apples and place in a large preserving pot. Add water, cover, and simmer until fruit is soft, stirring occasionally. Strain through a jelly bag [p. 28] and let drip for at least 4 or 5 hours.

Measure juice and cook 4 cups (1 L) at a time in a large stainless-steel pot. Cover and bring to a boil. Stir in 3/4 cup (175 mL) sugar to each cup (250 mL) juice. Bring to a rolling boil. Skimming as necessary, boil, uncovered, for about 15 minutes or less, until a small amount sheets off a metal spoon [p. 28-29]. The time it takes to make jelly varies with apple types and the season, but do not boil more than 15 minutes.

Remove jelly from heat and let subside. Stir, skimming if desired. Fill hot scalded jars [p. 28] to 1 /4 inch (5 mm) from the top and seal at once with snap lids and screw bands, and seal. Process in a boiling-water bath [p. 26] or steam canner for 10 minutes.

Variations: To make *apple-mint jelly,* add mint essence to each batch of juice. Prepare essence: In a cup, cover well-packed peppermint leaves with boiling water and let steep for several hours. Press down leaves with back of a spoon to extract all flavor. Strain and set aside 2 Tbsp (25 mL) mint juice, or essence. Add 2 Tbsp (25 mL) to each batch of apple juice after it has been brought to a boil a second time. Proceed as above.

To make *apple-rose geranium jelly,* use reddish-green apples and proceed as above, adding 3 rose geranium leaves to each batch of juice. Remove leaves before jarring and sealing.

To make *apple-spice jelly,* add 2 whole cloves, tied up in a muslin or cheesecloth bag, to every batch of juice. Bring to a boil and stir in 4 cups (1 L) sugar and 1/2 cup (125 mL) vinegar. Proceed as above, removing cloves before jarring and sealing.

Apple Ginger

I make this every year to sell at fall craft sales and it always sells out. It is an old recipe that I discovered when a friend gave me some preserved ginger as a gift and I looked for ways to use it in preserving. The directions call for not only using the flesh of the apple, but the peelings and cores, to produce a very high pectin juice. Apple ginger is a beautiful amber color and the consistency of a spread, delicious with cream cheese on toast, crackers, or whatever. Use sweet, ripe early-fall apples. You can also use it as a glaze on roast chicken, pork, or ham.

Makes 3 to 4 pt (1.5 to 2 L)

3 lb apples (1.5 kg)
1/2 lb preserved ginger, cut up in small pieces (125 g)
Sugar

Pare and core apples; cut apples into small pieces. Place parings and cores in a large preserving pot. Cover with water and simmer, covered, until soft, stirring occasionally. Strain.

Measure juice and pour into a large stainless-steel pot. Stir in 1 cup (250 mL) sugar to every 1 1/2 cups (375 mL) juice. Stir in cut-up apples and 3 more cups (750 mL) sugar. Stir in preserved ginger; increase amount for stronger ginger flavor. Simmer, uncovered, until thick, stirring as necessary.

Remove apple ginger from heat. Pour into hot scalded jars [p. 28], leaving 1/4 inch (5 mm) headroom, and seal at once with snap lids and screw bands. Process in a boiling-water bath [p. 26] or steam canner for 15 minutes.

Note: Preserved ginger can be found in supermarkets next to candied citron (it is already cut up in small pieces), or in specialty food stores, where the preserved ginger may be in larger pieces.

Apple Sweetmeats

This makes a chunky applesauce that is sweet enough to retain its original name. Use large, hard, early-fall apples.

Makes about 3 qt (3 L)

3 cups sugar (750 mL)
4 to 5 lb unpeeled apple slices (2 to 2.5 kg)
1 qt water (1 L)
Cinnamon

In a large preserving pot, combine sugar and water, stirring to dissolve sugar. Bring to a boil. Drop in apple slices. Simmer mixture, uncovered, until slices are soft.

Remove sweetmeats from heat and add cinnamon to taste. Ladle into hot scalded canning jars [p. 28], leaving 1/2 inch (1 cm) headroom. Adjust lids and process jars in a boiling-water bath [p. 26] or steam canner for 20 minutes.

Old-Fashioned Applesauce

Today, there is a whole generation that does not know that applesauce can be made with just a hand food mill. Here is that old-fashioned, time-honored way. Use large amounts of apples: small ones, big ones, and blemished ones.

Makes about 1 qt (1 L)

3 to 4 lb apples (1.5 to 2 kg)
Cinnamon
Sugar

Cut up apples, without skinning or coring or trimming too fastidiously. Place in a large preserving pot, adding a little water to prevent scorching. Simmer, covered, until soft, adding more water if apples seem dry. Put mixture through a food mill and stir in sugar and cinnamon to taste. Reheat to boiling point.

Remove applesauce from heat. Pour into hot scalded canning jars [p. 28], leaving 1/2 inch (1 cm) headroom. Adjust lids and process jars in a boiling-water bath [p. 26] or steam canner for 20 minutes.

Apple Butter I

WHEN MAKING APPLE BUTTER, TRY TO FIND CIDER MADE FROM RUSSET APPLES. OTHERWISE, USE THE SWEETEST CIDER AVAILABLE. THE RESULT SHOULD BE A PLEASANT REDDISH-BROWN.

Makes about 8 pt (4 L)

8 qt apples (8 L)
3 lb sugar (1.5 kg)
2 qt cider (2 L)
3 tsp cinnamon (15 ml)
4 qt water (4 L)
1 1/2 tsp cloves (7 mL)

Cut apples into small pieces and place in a large preserving pot. Add cider and water. Stirring occasionally, simmer mixture, covered, until apples are soft. Put through a food mill.

Place pulp in a large preserving pot. Add sugar, cinnamon, and cloves. Stirring frequently with a wooden spoon, cook pulp slowly, uncovered, until very thick.

Remove butter from heat. Pour into hot scalded jars [p. 28], leaving 1/4 inch (5 mm) headroom, and seal at once with snap lids and screw bands. Process in a boiling-water bath [p. 26] or steam canner for 10 minutes.

Apple Pectin

MAKE THIS EARLY IN THE SEASON, WITH TART, JUICY APPLES. FOR MAKING JELLY FROM LOW PECTIN FRUITS, USE EQUAL AMOUNT OF APPLE PECTIN TO EXTRACTED JUICE, AND 1/2 CUP SUGAR (175 ML) FOR EVERY 1 CUP (250 ML) OF COMBINED JUICES.

Makes about 2 pt (1 L)

2 lb apples (1 kg)
2 Tbsp lemon juice (25 mL)
1 qt water (1 L)

Cut up apples without peeling or coring, and place in a large preserving pot. Add water, cover, add lemon juice, and simmer until apples are soft, about 40 minutes, stirring occasionally. Strain mixture through a jelly bag [p. 28] and let drip overnight.

In a large stainless-steel pot, bring juice to a rolling boil and cook, uncovered, for 15 minutes.

Remove pectin from heat. Pour into hot scalded canning jars [p. 28], leaving 1/2 inch (1 cm) headroom, and adjust lids. Process in a boiling-water bath [p. 26) or steam canner for 10 minutes.

Apple Butter II

THIS BUTTER IS DIFFERENT ENOUGH FROM APPLE BUTTER I THAT IT DESERVES A SEPARATE NAME. USE THE SWEETEST APPLES AVAILABLE.

Makes 2 1/2 pt (1.25 L)

2 qt peeled apple quarters (2 L)
1 1/2 tsp cinnamon (7 mL)
2 qt sweet cider (2 L)
1/2 tsp cloves (2 mL)
1 1/2 cups sugar (375 mL)
1/2 tsp allspice (2 mL)

In a large preserving pot, combine apple quarters and cider. Cook slowly for about 2 hours, stirring occasionally. Add sugar, cinnamon, cloves, and allspice. Continue cooking slowly until thick. Remove butter from heat. Jar, seal, and process as for Apple Butter I.

Apple Crisp

Serves 6

6 apples
2 Tbsp sugar (25 mL)
1/4 tsp cinnamon (1 mL)
1 Tbsp white wine, cider, elderberry sass [p.128], or water (15 mL)
1/3 cup butter (80 mL)
1/3 cup brown sugar (80 mL)
3/4 cup flour (177 mL)

Generously butter a medium-sized bread pan. Core and thinly slice apples but do not peel. Fill bread pan almost to top. Sprinkle granulated sugar and cinnamon over apples; add white wine, cider, elderberry sass, or water if apples are dry.

In a bowl, make a crumb mixture by rubbing together butter, brown sugar, and flour. Sprinkle over apples and pat down to form a cover. Bake apple crisp in a 325°F (160°C) oven for about 1 hour or until apples are tender. Serve cold or hot with cream.

Apple Cider

This isn't really a recipe. But if you ever have bushels and bushels of apples around and you don't know what to do with them—have them turned into cider. We used to put down four barrels of cider every fall. One was for vinegar and the others for drinking throughout the year.

To make apple cider, you have to have a cider press and chopper. Or if you live in an area where there is a cider mill, you can pay to have your apples pressed. A bushel of apples will usually yield about 3 gallons (12 L) juice. Any kind of apples can be used— wildings or imperfect ones—but some types (Russet) are juicier and sweeter and make better cider. (To preserve sweet cider, freeze it in milk cartons or similar containers.)

If you want hard, or alcoholic, cider, plan on making a barrelful, which will require 15 to 20 bushels of apples. Put the juice in a charred oak barrel, the best kind for aging hard cider. Roll the barrel down cellar and place it on its side, up on blocks so that it's about 1 ft (30 cm) off the floor. Make sure the side with the bung hole is up. Drill a 1/3-inch (1-cm) hole straight through the bung and insert a 12-inch (30-cm) piece of plastic tubing. Place a glass of water beside the bung and run the other end of the tube into it, to form an air lock, allowing bubbles from fermentation to escape but preventing air from entering the barrel.

When you want to tap the barrel, drill a 1-inch (2.5-cm) hole through the top of the barrel about 2 1/2 inches (6 cm) from the bottom edge. Quickly drive in a spigot. Hard cider is best 9 or 10 months after it has been put down, when it is pale gold and tastes like a fine fruity dry wine.

Apple Leather

This is a wonderful way to use an abundance of apples, particularly less-perfect ones.

Cut up any amount of apples. Trim them but not too meticulously. Place in a large preserving pot. Add a little water, only enough to prevent scorching. Cover, bring to a boil, stirring often. Uncover and simmer until apples are soft. Put mixture through a food mill. Add honey or corn syrup to taste if desired.

Spread pulp thinly on cookie sheets lined with one layer of heavy plastic wrap. Set pans in sun or in a just-warm oven or on top of a woodstove.

Turn fruit when it can be lifted off plastic without falling apart; it should be barely sticky to touch and still pliable. Remove plastic and dry other side of leather. Roll up leather in fresh plastic and store in jars or crocks. To use, unroll and cut off pieces with scissors.

Note: Honey seems to make a softer, more pliable leather, but it does mask the apple taste. Sweetener is really unnecessary because the fruit is condensed, and, as a result, its natural sweet flavor is intensified.

Curdie's Apple-Crumb Pie

This is a Mennonite recipe that our daughter has made her own. It calls for tart apples and a hefty amount of sugar, so if you use sweet apples, you may want to reduce the sugar. Whatever you prefer.

6 to 8 tart apples
1 tsp cinnamon (5 mL)
Pastry [p. 46]
3/4 cup flour (275 mL)
1 cup sugar (250 mL)
1/3 cup butter (75 mL)

Core and thinly slice apples but do not peel. Generously fill a 9-inch (1-L) pie plate with cut-up apples and then remove them. Place in a bowl and line pie plate with pastry.

In a separate bowl, mix together 1/2 cup (125 mL) sugar and cinnamon; mix into apples. Pour mixture into pie shell.

Combine remaining sugar and flour. Add butter and rub mixture together until it forms crumbs. Sprinkle over apples. Bake pie in a 350°F (180°C) oven for about 45 minutes.

Note: If using dry apples, add some thinned elderberry sass [p. 121] to the apple mixture to make the pie juicier.

Applesauce Cake

This is a wonderfully moist cake that improves with age.

1/2 cup butter, shortening, or lard (125 mL)
1 cup nuts (250 mL)
1 cup chopped raisins and black currants 250 mL
3/4 cup sugar (175 ml,)
1 egg, well beaten
1/2 tsp cinnamon (2 mL)
1 tsp vanilla (5 mL)
1/4 tsp cloves (1 mL)
1 cup chopped dates (250 mL)
2 cups unbleached all-purpose flour (500 mL)
1 1/2 cups unsweetened applesauce (375 mL)
2 tsp baking soda (10 mL)

In a bowl, cream butter and add sugar; beat well. Add well-beaten egg, vanilla, and remaining ingredients. Blend. Pour batter into a greased 9-inch (2.5-L) springform pan. Bake in a 350°F (180°C) oven for about 1 hour or until a knife or cake tester inserted in center comes out clean.

Note: To make with canned sweetened applesauce [p. 152], reduce amount of sugar to 1/4 to 1/2 cup (50 to 125 mL).

A bowl of applesauce

Easy Apple Cake

This cake is made for the Jewish Sabbath in the religious community Aish Ha Torah in Jerusalem and it has become our favorite apple cake. It's kosher, which means that it can be served with either meat or dairy meals in an observant Jewish home. Use large sweet, juicy firm apples.

3 cups unpeeled apple slices
3 tsp baking powder (15 mL)
1 Tbsp cinnamon (15 mL)
4 eggs
1 3/4 cups sugar (425 mL)
1/4 cup orange juice (50 mL)
3 cups flour (750 mL)
1 Tbsp vanilla (15 mL)
1 tsp salt (5 mL)
1 cup salad oil (250 mL)

Place apple slices in a bowl. Stir in cinnamon and 4 Tbsp (75 mL) sugar.

In a large bowl, combine remaining sugar, flour, salt, and baking powder. Make a well in center and add eggs, orange juice, vanilla, and oil. Beat mixture until smooth.

Lightly grease a 9-inch (2.5-mL) springform pan. Spread one-third of dough on bottom of pan. Add half of apple slices and arrange evenly over top of dough. Cover apples with one-third of dough. Arrange rest of apple slices on top and cover with remaining dough.

Bake in a 350°F (180°C) oven for 75 minutes or until knife or cake tester inserted in center comes out clean. During baking, cover cake with tin foil for 20 minutes so it doesn't dry out.

Applesauce Muffins

Very moist.

Makes 1 dozen

2 cups unbleached all-purpose flour (500 mL)
1 egg, lightly beaten
2 Tbsp melted butter (25 mL)
3/4 tsp salt (4 mL)
1 cup sweetened applesauce [p. 152] (250 mL)
3 Tbsp sugar (50 mL)
3 tsp baking powder (15 mL)
1/2 cup milk (125 mL)
1/2 tsp cinnamon (2 mL)

Sift together flour, salt, sugar, baking powder, and cinnamon. Make a well in center. Add egg, butter, and applesauce; blend well. Stir in enough milk to make a smooth, creamy batter. Spoon into greased muffin tins and bake in a 400°F (200°C) oven for about 20 minutes.

Crabapples

If you plant crabapples, keep in mind that the prettiest-flowering varieties do not generally bear the best fruit for preserving. Wild crabapples are fine to use for jelly, marmalade, preserves, and sauce.

Crabapple Jelly

Crabapples are high in pectin, so they make a fast-setting jelly. Take care not to overcook! Include crabapple juice in jellies using fruits low in pectin (elderberries, for example.)

1 qt (1 L) juice makes about 2 pt (1 L)

Crabapples
Sugar

Halve larger crabapples. In a large preserving pot, cover at least 3 lb (1.5 kg) crabapples with cold water. Bring to a boil and reduce heat. Stirring occasionally, simmer, covered, until crabapples are soft. Strain mixture through a jelly bag [p. 28] and let drip for at least 5 hours.

Measure juice and cook 4 cups (1 L) at a time in a large stainless-steel pot. Cover and bring to a boil. Stir in 1 cup (250 mL) sugar to each cup (250 mL) juice. Bring to a rolling boil. Skimming as necessary, boil, uncovered, for about 10-15 minutes or until a small amount sheets off a metal spoon [p. 28-29].

Remove jelly from heat and let subside. Stir, skimming if desired. Fill hot scalded jars [p. 28] to 1/4 inch (5 mm) from the top and seal at once with snap lids and screw bands. Process in a boiling-water bath [p. 28] or steam canner for 10 minutes.

Crabapple Marmalade

THIS IS AN OLD RECIPE THAT YOU WILL NEVER FIND IN MODERN COOKBOOKS. THAT'S UNFORTUNATE BECAUSE THIS MARMALADE HAS CHARACTER AND DISTINCTION—TANGY IN TASTE AND ROSE VELVET IN COLOR.

Makes 6 pt (3 L)

6 lb crabapples (3 kg)
1 pt vinegar (500 mL)
2 oranges
2 tsp ground cloves (10 mL)
12 scant cups sugar (3 L)
2 tsp ground cinnamon (10 mL)

Halve larger crabapples. In a large preserving pot, combine crab-apples and a little water. Simmer, covered, until soft.

Meanwhile, cut oranges into quarters, removing and setting aside peel. Cut up orange quarters, removing seeds. In a small pot, simmer peel in water, covered, until soft. Drain, remove white skin, and cut into small pieces.

Put crabapple mixture through a food mill and place in a stainless-steel pot. Add sugar, vinegar, spices, orange pieces, and prepared peel. Stirring often, simmer mixture, uncovered, until thick.

Remove marmalade from heat and let subside. Stir. Fill hot scalded jars [p. 28] to 1/4 inch (5 mm) from the top and seal at once with snap lids and screw bands. Process in a boiling-water bath [p. 26] or steam canner for 10 minutes.

Crabapple Preserves

EAT THESE PRESERVES AS A DELICACY WITH ANY MEAL, EITHER AS A DESSERT OR AS A CONDIMENT, BY HOLDING ON TO THE STEMS AND DISCARDING THE SEEDS ONTO YOUR PLATE. DON'T FORGET TO EAT THE SYRUP.

Makes 5 to 6 pt (2.5 to 3 L)

Heavy Syrup:

6 lb crabapples (3 kg)
3 lb sugar (1.5 kg)
2 cups water (500 mL)

In a large preserving pot, dissolve sugar in water. Bring mixture to a boil, covered. Boil for a few minutes and add crabapples, carefully stirring with a long-handled fork to prevent damage. Bring to a boil and simmer, uncovered, for 5 minutes, stirring as necessary.

Remove preserves from heat. Ladle into hot scalded jars [p. 28], fill with syrup, leaving 1/2 inch headroom and seal at once with snap lids and screw bands. Process in a boiling-water bath [p. 26] or steam canner for 15 minutes.

Variation: To make *crabapple sauce,* bring preserves to a boil, covered. Put through a food mill, syrup and all. Serve with anything, adding cream if you like.

Peaches

No longer do northern gardeners have to pine for peaches. Reliance is dependably hardy to Zone 4, and although the fruit is small, flavor is intense. Many good varieties are available in warmer growing zones. Standard trees grow up to 15 feet (4.6 m) and have to be planted 20 ft apart (6.1 m). If space is a problem, look for semi-dwarf types that grow up to about 8 to 10 ft (2.4 to 3.0 m) and are planted 10 ft apart (3.0 m). Both are self-pollinating. If you can't grow your own peaches, superior tasting, good quality fruit is available at fruit stands in the summer. Better ask to taste one before you buy, though. In rainy years, peaches can be mealy and very poor for preserving. Sweet, firm, and juicy peaches are what you want. And freestone, otherwise you will have a miserable time separating fruit from pits. Be sure to add peaches to the brandied-fruit crock.

Nellie's Peach Jam

This simple recipe was developed by our busy daughter, Nell. She likes to preserve, but she doesn't have a lot of time, so when she does make jam, she wants it to come out well without a lot of fuss. She says she never thought about adding additional pectin, since the peaches jell fast on their own. She uses the same proportion of fruit to sugar as for Raspberry Jam [p.67] and adds lemon juice to keep the cut-up peaches from discoloring while she's peeling them. Use firm, ripe peaches.

Makes about 1 1/2 pt (700 mL)

1 quart cut-up and peeled peaches, about 10 good-sized (1 L)
3 cups sugar (700 mL)
Lemon juice

To remove skins: immerse fruit in boiling water up to 1 minute, then plunge into ice water; slip off skins, halve each peach, remove pit, and cut up into medium chunks. Squeeze lemon juice over chunks so they don't discolor while you are preparing more fruit. Place cut-up peaches in a large stainless-steel pot, then mash the chunks to speed cooking (Nell says they break down easily). Cook fruit, covered, and when simmering, remove cover, stir in sugar. Bring to a rolling boil and cook, stirring often, about 10 minutes or until mixture thickens. Remove pot from heat. Fill hot scalded jars [p. 28] to 1/4 inch (5 mm) from the top and seal at once with snap lids and screw bands. Process in a boiling-water bath [p. 26] or steam canner for 15 minutes.

Ginger-Peach Jam

Bob Miller and his late wife Donna Brooks were early followers of the original edition of this book and innovative fruit preservers, as well as fruit growers. When Bob gave us a jar of this jam, we were impressed with its flavor and texture. He says he got it from the website Food.com where it is credited to Mirj. He made a few changes, which I have noted below. I am ever impressed with students who lead the teacher.

Makes about 2 1/2 pt (1.25 L)

2 lb peaches (about 6 cups) (0.9 kg)
3 cups sugar (700 mL)
3 1/2 Tbsp grated ginger (50 mL)
2 Tbsp lemon juice (30 mL)
1/4 tsp allspice (1 mL)

Place peaches in boiling water for one minute. Plunge them into ice water. Slip off skins, halve fruit and remove pits. Cut peaches into small pieces. In a large stainless-steel pot mix all ingredients and simmer about 30 minutes or until mixture thickens and mounds on a spoon. Remove pot from heat. Fill hot scalded jars [p. 28] to 1/4 inch (5 mm) from the top and seal at once with snap lids and screw bands. Process in a boiling-water bath [p. 26] or steam canner for 15 minutes.

Peach-Orange Marmalade

I amended this recipe from a bag of sugar, and contrary to my expectations, it's not too sweet. The addition of oranges speeds jelling. Use firm, ripe peaches.

Makes about 2 1/2 pt (1.25 L)

3 large juice oranges
1 lemon
3 lb peaches, about 12 medium (1.5 kg)
6 cups sugar (1.5 L)

Grate rinds of oranges and the lemon. Squeeze juices and remove seeds (don't strain). Peel peaches (optional) as for peach jam and cut up into small pieces. Put cut-up peaches in large stainless-steel pot, add citrus juices and grated rind. Stir in sugar, and bring mixture bring to a boil, uncovered, stirring to prevent sticking. Reduce heat and let simmer slowly until thickened, about 35-45 minutes. Remove pot from heat. Fill hot scalded jars [p. 28] to 1/4 inch (5 mm) from the top and seal at once with snap lids and screw bands. Process in a boiling-water bath [p. 26] or steam canner for 15 minutes.

Peach Butter

Use dead-ripe or overripe juicy peaches for this delicious butter.

Makes about 5 pt (2.5 L)

4 lb peaches (2 kg)
Cloves
Sugar
Cinnamon
Allspice

Cut up peaches but do not peel. Place in a large preserving pot and add enough water to prevent scorching. Simmer, covered, until fruit is tender. Put peaches through a food mill. Add 1/2 cup (125 mL) sugar to each cup (250 mL) pulp. Add spices to taste if desired.

In a large stainless-steel pot, cook mixture slowly, uncovered, until thick, stirring often to prevent sticking.

Remove butter from heat. Pour into hot scalded jars [p. 28], leaving 1/4 inch (5 mm) headroom, and seal at once with snap lids and screw bands. Process in a boiling-water bath [p. 26] or steam canner for 10 minutes.

Note: You can turn any excess fruit—grapes, pears, plums, cherries—into butters by following the above recipe. Less-juicy fruits require more water, up to 1 cup (250 mL) to each cup (250 ml) pulp.

Canned Peaches

Sweet, ripe peaches, canned in a light syrup, are the glory of the winter pantry, delicious by themselves or mixed with a variety of preserved fruits, especially strawberries. I no longer remove skins before adding to the syrup, an innovation I hope earns followers, since I detect no difference in the finished product and a lot of time and mess saved to devote to something more enjoyable. Of course, be sure to wash fruit well.

About 6 qt (6 L)

10 medium-large peaches (should make 1 qt/1 L of pieces)
Sugar

Quarter peaches and cut up in bite-size pieces. As you work, drop pieces into 1 gallon (3 L) water with 2 Tbsp (15 mL) salt to prevent discoloring. Add 1/2 cup (125 mL) sugar for each quart (1 L) of cut up fruit. Let sit to draw out juices, then heat fruit to boiling point in a large preserving pot, covered. Fill hot scalded jars [p. 28] to 1/2 inch (1 cm) from the top and seal at once with snap lids and screw bands. Process in a boiling-water bath [p. 26] or steam canner for 25 minutes.

Peach Leather

Use ripe fruit in any condition. Trim blemished parts. Cut peaches in half, remove pits, and chop peach halves into small pieces. Place in a large preserving pot, adding water if necessary. Simmer until fruit is soft, about 10 minutes, stirring in sugar or honey to taste if desired. Put mixture through a food mill. Spread pulp thinly on cookie sheets lined with one layer of heavy plastic wrap. Set pans in sun or in a just-warm oven or on top of a woodstove.

Turn fruit when it can be lifted off plastic without falling apart; it should be barely sticky to touch and still pliable. Remove plastic and dry other side of leather. Roll up leather in fresh plastic and store in jars or crocks. To use, unroll and cut off pieces with scissors.

Pears

The world of pears now includes Asian pears, round, juicy, and crisp, and best for eating fresh. The best variety for preserving is Bartlett, the one commonly available in grocery stores. Max-Red, a sport, is reported to be sweeter. Note that pears require two different types for proper pollination. Standard types grow from 18 to 20 ft tall (5.5 to 6.1 m) and should be spaced 20

Canned peaches in an upscale European canning jar

to 25 ft apart (6.1 to 7.6 m). As with all the dwarf types, dwarf pears are a blessing for those with less space to devote to fruit trees: they reach 8 to 10 ft tall (2.4 to 3.0 m) and should be planted 10 ft (3.0 m) apart. Wild or neglected pear trees often bear small hard fruit. It depends on the type, but pears usually need to be stored in a cool place before they are usable. Sometimes it's for as little as a few days; sometimes it's for as long as a couple of months.

Plain Pear Preserves

Canned pears are not overly sweet if they are preserved in a thin or moderate syrup. When I make pear preserves, I don't peel the fruit, although most people do. Here is the preferred method, but try mine sometime, too. Use Bartlett pears or another hard variety.

Pears

Light syrup:

1 qt water (1 L)
2 cups sugar (500 mL)

Peel, halve, and core pears. Prepare syrup. In a large preserving pot, boil together sugar and water, stirring to dissolve sugar. Add pears and simmer mixture for 5 minutes.

Pack pears into hot scalded canning jars [p. 28] and pour 1/2 to 1 cup (125 to 250 mL) syrup over pears, leaving 1/2 inch (1 cm) headroom. Adjust lids and process jars in a boiling-water bath [p. 26] or steam canner. Process 1-pt (50-mL) jars for 20 minutes, 1-qt (1-L) jars for 25 minutes.

Pears-in-Wine

Makes 1 1/2 pt (750 mL)

6 pears
1 piece cinnamon stick
1 cup sugar (250 mL)
1 slice lemon
1/2 cup elderberry wine [p. 125] or other red wine (225 mL)

Peel and core sweet, firm ripe pears; halve if large. In a large stainless-steel pot, combine sugar, wine, cinnamon, and lemon. Bring to a boil. Reduce heat and drop in pears. Cook over medium heat until fruit is tender. *Do not overcook.*

Discard cinnamon. Fill hot scalded jars [p. 28] with pears and pour 1/2 to 1 cup (125 to 250 mL) syrup over them, leaving 1/2 inch (1 cm) headroom. Make sure pears are covered with syrup. Seal at once with snap lids and screw bands. Process in a boiling-water bath [p. 26] or steam canner for 15 minutes.

Dried Pears

Pears are one of the easiest fruits to dry, and the result is very sweet.

Slice pears vertically, leaving skin and seeds to retain flavor. Lay thin slabs on a tray or cookie sheet lined with heavy plastic wrap. Place tray near cooking area, where it will receive extra heat, or in direct sunlight. Turn fruit daily.

To hasten drying, put tray in oven after heat has been turned off or in a just-warm oven. When they feel dry and pliable, pears are done. Store in covered crocks or jars.

Pear Leather

Chop overripe pears into small pieces, peel and all. Place in a large preserving pot, cover, and simmer until soft. Add water if necessary, to prevent scorching. Add sugar to taste if desired. Put mixture through a food mill.

Spread pulp thinly on cookie sheets lined with one layer of heavy plastic wrap. Set pans in sun or in a just-warm oven or on top of a woodstove.

Turn fruit when it can be lifted off plastic without falling apart; it should be barely sticky to touch and still pliable. Remove plastic and dry other side of leather. Roll up leather in fresh plastic and store in jars or crocks. To use, unroll and cut off pieces with scissors.

Plums

Of all tree fruits, plums are the easiest for the home gardener to grow and they are beautiful in bloom. Plum trees like heavy soil, and they produce abundant crops sooner than other fruit trees. Some varieties, though, are hardier and more disease resistant. Japanese plums require two different varieties for proper pollination. You could plant two different types anyway, one for preserving and one for eating fresh. As with other fruit trees, dwarf types are available if you are cramped for growing space: Dwarf plum trees grow from 8 to 10 ft tall (2.4 to 3.0 m) and should be planted 10 ft apart (3.0 m); standard types reach 15 ft (4.6 m) and should be planted 20 ft apart (6.1 m). Plum varieties are constantly subject to change, so if you are interested in growing them, consult your local Cooperative Extension for recommended types (see Appendix).

Plum Preserves

This is an easy way to preserve a lot of plums if you are lucky enough to be overwhelmed by them, as we are on occasion. The pits are left in, so beware when you eat them. Use firm, not overripe, plums, preferably a preserving variety, such as Damson.

Makes about 1 qt (1 L)

Heavy syrup:

1 1/2 to 2 lb plums (750 g to 1 kg)
3/4 cup sugar (175 mL)
1/2 cup water (125 mL)

Prepare syrup. In a large stainless-steel pot, stir sugar into water. Cover and bring to a boil, stirring as necessary. Add plums and simmer, uncovered, for 5 minutes, stirring carefully with a long-handled fork, only as necessary.

Remove preserves from heat. Ladle into hot scalded jars [p. 28], leaving 1/2 inch (1 cm) headroom, and seal at once with snap lids and screw bands. Process in a boiling-water bath [p. 26] or steam canner for 15 minutes.

Note: Always do plums in small batches to keep them from breaking down. You can also use the above recipe for making cherry preserves.

Plum Jam

THIS IS A KNOCKOUT ON VANILLA ICE CREAM.

Makes 1 pt (500 mL)

Plums

Sugar

If plums are freestone, remove pits before cooking. Otherwise, in a large stainless-steel pot, combine plums and a small amount of water. Simmer, covered, until soft. Cool mixture and remove pits.

Simmer plums, uncovered, until they form a pulp that is fairly thick and measures 2 cups (500 mL). Add 1 1/2 cups (375 mL) sugar, stir often, and simmer until mixture thickens.

Remove jam from heat and let subside. Stir. Fill hot scalded jars [p. 28] to 1/4 inch (5 mm) from the top and seal at once with snap lids and screw bands. Process in a boiling-water bath [p. 26] or steam canner for 15 minutes.

Quince

Quince is a small, graceful tree with grayish bark, crooked stems, goblet-like white flowers in late spring, and if you're lucky, perfumed golden fruit that hangs at the tips of its branches by fall. Even if I never got a single fruit, I would want to grow fruiting quince (*Cydonia oblonga*) for its old-fashioned aura and ornamental qualities (not as showy as flowering quince, *Chaenomeles* spp., but elegant in its way). Fruiting quince grows to 10 to 12 ft (3.0 to 3.7 m) so it can easily be tucked into a shrub border as long as it receives a half day of full sun. It grows best, and is less prone to disease, in a site with good air circulation. It is self-pollinating, will grow in most soils, and is hardy to -25° F (-32° C). Quinces are high in Vitamin C and pectin-rich, so their extracted juice helps low-pectin fruit to jell. They are known for their affinity for apples in any form. Add a few small, cut-up pieces to applesauce and apple pies to impart their distinct flavor. See Appendix for these hard-to-find fruit trees.

Wild Fruits

Before we owned a farm, we made seasonal forays to pick wild berries because we wanted to add more fruit to our diet and our income was very limited. Like a little army of squirrels, we packed into the old Dodge truck and came home with buckets of fruit. Before

Quince Jelly

This is a beautiful pink color and slightly tart.

Quince
Sugar

Wipe fuzz from fruits. Cut up in small pieces, nearly cover with water, bring to a boil and simmer, with the cover tilted, for about 2 hours until quite tender. Drain through a jelly bag overnight [p. 28]. Measure juice and cook 4 cups (1 L) at a time in a large stainless-steel pot. Cover and bring to a boil. Stir in 1 cup (250 mL) sugar to each cup (250 mL) juice. Bring to a rolling boil. Skimming as necessary, boil, uncovered, for about 10-15 minutes or until a small amount sheets off a metal spoon [p. 28-29]. Remove jelly from heat and let subside. Stir, skimming if desired. Fill hot scalded jars [p. 28] to 1/4 inch (5 mm) from the top and seal at once with snap lids and screw bands. Process in a boiling-water bath [p. 26] or steam canner for 10 minutes.

Quince Paste

Pastes are a more condensed form of fruit butters. You should be able to cut a fruit paste into little squares. There are many old recipes for making quince paste. This one comes from Jeanne Leblanc, who learned about quince paste on a visit to Spain, and likes to serve it on toast or rice crackers with a thin slice of goat gouda.

Peel, core, and quarter at least 6 large quinces. (Jeanne says that the core seeds tend to gum up the food mill, and little flecks of skin remain in the purée, which is ok if you like it that way.) Put the pieces in a large preserving pot and add water to cover. Bring to a boil and simmer until quinces are soft, which may take up to 45 minutes. Drain, cool, and run through a food mill to make a purée.

Put the purée in a large pot, place over medium heat and add an equal amount of sugar by volume. Bring the mixture to a boil, reduce to a simmer and cook, stirring regularly, until it darkens slightly and thickens. The purée is ready when it quickly clots on a frozen plate, when a wooden spoon stands up in the pot, or when the purée drips in sheets from the spoon. This usually takes about 30 minutes.

Pour the hot, sweetened purée into a bowl or mold and leave to set for at least 24 hours. Unmold when ready to eat. Slice and serve.

Refrigerate the remaining quince paste for up to 3 months. Jeanne preserves hers like any jam and processes it for 5 minutes in a boiling-water bath [p. 26]. She sometimes freezes some purée so she can thaw it, add sugar, and make more quince paste during the year.

the first frost, we always remembered to get some sumac stalks, too, to flavor winter drinks.

Later, we lived on a remote back-country farm without any vehicle at all. We got almost all our fruit from what we planted, except for an annual expedition to the local shore for cranberries. Occasionally, we enjoyed a harvest of chokecherries from bushes the birds so thoughtfully planted along the 1/2 mile lane into our farm. Wherever we live, though, we continue to explore the wild for edible fruits.

Barberries

Early settlers first brought the tart barberry (*Berberis vulgaris*) to New England. Barberries are still found in New England, growing along banks or wherever escapees find conditions favorable. The attractive, but thorny, bushes bear long clusters of juicy, oblong, brilliant orange-red berries, usually harvested in the early fall. A domesticated ornamental variety, *Berberis thunbergii,* bears inedible fruit and in some areas is considered invasive.

Blackberries

Blackberries grow wild over much of North America, but the farther south you go, the bigger and juicier the berries get. In warm climates, they grow in large thickets, and you can spend days picking them by the bucket, for jam or for syrup or to eat fresh with other fruits (particularly peaches) and lots of thick cream. Breeders appear to have been busy with blackberries. If you want to grow them, look for new varieties that bear on first year canes (primocane bearing). These are Prime Jim, Prime Jan, and Prime Ark, hardy to Zone 4, because they can freeze to the ground over winter and still produce a crop the following summer. *Note:* Dewberries and closely related boysenberries, youngberries, and loganberries, can be used interchangeably in the recipes below.

Barberry Sauce

JIGS, EVER ON THE LOOK OUT FOR THE POSSIBILITIES OF EDIBLE WILD FRUITS, GOT THE IDEA FOR PRESERVING BARBERRIES FROM OUR NOW TATTERED FERNALD'S *EDIBLE WILD PLANTS OF EASTERN NORTH AMERICA*. THIS SAUCE IS MORE LIKE A CONFECTION—POPULAR WITH CHILDREN.

Barberries
Molasses

In a large stainless-steel pot, bring equal amounts of barberries and molasses to a boil, covered. Skim out barberries and boil syrup, uncovered, until reduced, by half. Make sure it does not burn. Add barberries and bring to a rolling boil.

Remove sauce from heat. Stir. Ladle into hot scalded jars [p. 28], leaving 1/4 inch (5 mm) headroom, and seal at once with snap lids and screw bands, and process in a boiling-water bath [p. 26] or steam canner for 15 minutes.

Blackberry Jam

Use a mixture of ripe and slightly underripe berries. The larger wild berries from the mid-Atlantic states and from the South make a less seedy jam.

Makes about 1 1/2 pt (750 mL)

1 qt blackberries (1 L)
3 cups sugar (750 mL)
2 Tbsp lemon juice (25 mL)

In a large stainless-steel pot, mash blackberries to expel juice. Bring to simmering point, covered. Stir in sugar and lemon juice. Stirring frequently, boil, uncovered, for about 15 minutes or less, or until mixture thickens and begins to cling to bottom of pot.

Remove jam from heat and let subside. Stir, skimming if desired. Fill hot scalded jars [p. 28] to 1/4 inch (5 mm) from the top and seal at once with snap lids and screw bands. Process in a boiling-water bath [p. 26] or steam canner for 15 minutes.

Note: For less-seedy jam, put part of cooked berries through a food mill before adding sugar.

Blackberry Syrup

YOU CAN MAKE JUICE FROM THIS SYRUP AS WELL—JUST DILUTE IT WITH WATER TO TASTE. USE DEAD-RIPE BLACKBERRIES. USE OVER ICE CREAM, ADD TO PIES, PRESERVES, OR FRUIT DISHES OF ANY KIND.

Makes 6 to 8 pt (3 to 4 L)

6 qt blackberries (6 L)
Sugar
2 1/2 qt water (2.5 L)

In a large preserving pot, mash blackberries. Add water, cover, and bring to a boil. Stirring occasionally, simmer for 10 minutes or until berries are soft and juice runs freely. Strain through a jelly bag [p. 28] and let drip for several hours or overnight.

Measure juice and cook 6 cups (1.5 L) at a time in a large stainless-steel pot. Bring to a boil, covered. Stir in 1/2 cup (125 mL) sugar to each cup (250 mL) juice. Boil, uncovered, for about 10 to 15 minutes or until mixture thickens.

Remove syrup from heat and let subside. Pour into hot scalded jars [p. 28], leaving 1/4 inch (5 mm) headroom, and seal at once with snap lids and screw bands. Process in a boiling-water bath [p. 26] or steam canner for 10 minutes.

Curdie's Blackberry Pie

INGENIOUS AND SIMPLE, THIS PIE IS A GREAT DESSERT FOR HOT MIDSUMMER DAYS. OUR DAUGHTER REMEMBERS IT WELL FROM VISITS TO A VERMONT FARM.

2 cups sugar (500 mL)
Baked pie shell [p. 46]
1 cup water (250 mL)
Whipped cream [p. 58]
1 qt blackberries (1 L)

In a pot, boil together sugar and water, uncovered, to form a syrup, about 5 minutes. Stir until sugar is dissolved. Pour over blackberries and place mixture in a baked 9-inch (23-cm) pie shell. Top with whipped cream and refrigerate until ready to serve.

Blueberries

Wild blueberries thrive in northern New England and eastern Canada, and when we have been unable to grow them, we always look for them in the wild. Sometimes, if we can't pick them, a friend picks them for us and we barter for some of Jigs' great smoked fish. The cultivated high-bush blueberry grows into a large shrub if given acid, well-drained soil and moderate moisture. There are a growing number of varieties available to the home gardener; some are self-pollinating, others need another variety for proper pollination. High-bush blueberries grow to 5 ft (1.5 m); plant them 4 ft (1.2 m) apart. On the farm we raised a long hedge of these and the plants were so heavily laden that we could not keep up with them and so invited friends to come and pick. They are beautiful at every stage, from flowering to fruiting, and in the fall, the foliage turns deep crimson. No wonder blueberries are popular plants. Breeders have been busy developing them for earlier ripening, hardiness, larger or tastier fruit. There are dwarf types for growing in tubs if you're limited for space. Because the berries don't all ripen at once, you will need several bushes to have enough to preserve. Watch out for birds, and net if you see damage. Blueberries, like black currants and elderberries, are high in Vitamin C and other health benefits.

Note: Huckleberries may be substituted for blueberries in any of these recipes.

Blueberry Preserves

Blueberries are one of the easiest fruits to can, and cooking them seems to bring out their flavor. Use firm ripe berries.

Blueberries
Sugar

In a large preserving pot, combine blueberries and sugar, using 1/4 to 1/2 cup (50 to 125 mL) sugar to each qt (L) blueberries. Bring to a boil, stirring frequently to prevent sticking.

Remove preserves from heat. Ladle into hot scalded canning jars [p. 28], leaving 1/2 inch (1 cm) headroom, and adjust lids. Process jars for 10 minutes in a boiling-water bath [p. 26] or steam canner.

Blueberry Jam

This is fast-setting with homemade apple pectin [p. 149].

Makes about 2 pt (1 L)

1 qt blueberries, some a little under-ripe (1 L)
1 cup apple pectin (250 mL)
2 Tbsp lemon juice (25 mL)
3 cups sugar (750 mL)

Heat berries, pectin and lemon juice to simmering, stir in sugar, and bring to a rolling boil. Boil hard for 10 minutes or until thickened. Remove jam from heat and let subside. Stir, skimming if desired. Fill hot scalded jars [p. 28] to 1/4 inch (5 mm) from the top and seal at once with snap lids and screw bands. Process in a boiling-water bath [p. 26] or steam canner for 15 minutes.

Blueberry Cobbler

1 qt blueberries (1 L)
1 Tbsp baking powder (15 mL)
1 cup sugar (250 mL)
1/4 tsp salt (1 mL)
1/4 cup melted butter (50 mL)
3 Tbsp shortening or lard (50 mL)
Juice of 1/2 a lemon
1 egg
1 cup cake flour 250 mL
1/4 cup milk 50 mL
Pinch nutmeg

Place blueberries, sugar, butter, and lemon juice in a greased baking dish. Mix.

Mix and sift together flour, nutmeg, baking powder, and salt. Cut in shortening with a pastry cutter until evenly distributed.

In a bowl, beat together egg and milk; stir into flour-shortening mixture. Drop spoonfuls of dough over blueberries to cover. Bake cobbler in a 350°F (180°C) oven for about 40 minutes or until dough is lightly browned and berries are bubbling.

Note: To make with blueberry preserves (above), reduce sugar to taste. Stir 1 heaping Tbsp (15 mL) flour into blueberry mixture and proceed.

Blueberry Cake

1/2 cup butter (125 mL)
1 tsp baking powder (5 mL)
3/4 cup sugar (175 mL)
1 1/2 cups blueberries (375 mL)
2 eggs, well beaten
1/3 cup milk (75 mL)
1 1/2 cups flour (375 mL)
1 tsp vanilla (5 mL)
Pinch salt

In a bowl, cream butter with sugar; add well-beaten eggs. Mix and sift together flour, salt, and baking powder; stir into butter-sugar mixture. Stir in blueberries. Add milk and stir mixture well but do not overheat. Add vanilla. Pour batter into a shallow buttered pan and bake in a 350° F (180°C) oven for 35 minutes or until cake is lightly browned and knife inserted in center comes out clean.

Vera's Blueberry Kolachky

A LONG TIME CZECH FRIEND ONCE MADE THIS WONDERFUL CONFECTION FOR US.

1/4 cup warm water (50 mL)
1 large egg, well beaten
1 tsp granulated sugar (5 mL)
3 cups flour (750 mL)
1/4 tsp ginger (1 mL)
Softened shortening or salad oil
Blueberries
1 Tbsp dry yeast (15 mL)
1/2 cup milk (125 mL)
1/4 cup butter (50 mL)

Topping:

1/3 cup sugar (75 mL)
1 cup brown sugar (250 mL)
1/2 tsp salt (2 mL)
1/2 cup cold butter (125 mL)
1/2 cup cold water (125 mL)
1 Tbsp cinnamon (15 mL)

In a large bowl, combine warm water, 1 tsp (5 mL) granulated sugar, ginger, and yeast. Let stand in a warm place until mixture is dissolved and yeast begins to foam.

In a saucepan, scald milk, stirring in butter until melted. Dissolve 1/3 cup (75 mL) sugar and salt in hot milk. Remove from heat. Stir in cold water to cool milk mixture to warm; add to yeast mixture. Add well-beaten egg and 1 cup (250 mL) flour. Beat well. Mix in remaining flour or enough to get dough to clear bowl.

Place dough on a board sprinkled with flour and cover with bowl, turned upside down. Let dough rest at least 5 minutes. Then knead until smooth and elastic, adding more flour if necessary to make a smooth, satiny dough. Return dough to bowl and brush top of it with softened shortening or a little salad oil. Cover bowl with a towel and leave dough to double in bulk.

Punch down dough. Place in a 10-inch x 14-inch (4-L) pan, flattening dough to fit bottom of pan and pulling it up along sides to form a rim. Fill depressed dough with fresh blueberries, right up to rim.

Prepare topping. In a bowl, mix together brown sugar, cold butter, and cinnamon. Work the mixture until it forms coarse crumbs. Sprinkle over blueberries.

Let kolachky rise until light and bake in a 350°F (180°C) oven for about 20 minutes or until dough is firm and blueberries are bubbling.

Cape Breton Blueberry Muffins

I AM INDEBTED TO THE *CAPE BRETON BICENTENNIAL DANCERS* COOKBOOK OF FAVORITE RECIPES FOR THESE BEST-EVER MUFFINS.

Makes about 15

1 cup sugar (250 mL)
2 eggs
1/2 cup butter or margarine (125 mL 2) cups flour 500 mL
2 tsp baking powder (10 mL)
1/2 tsp salt (2 mL)
1/2 cup milk (125 mL)
2 1/2 cups blueberries, fresh or frozen (625 mL)

Cream sugar, butter, and eggs. Mix flour, baking powder, and salt. Add alternately with milk. Mix until just smooth. Add blueberries, lightly dusted with a little of the flour mixture so they don't sink to the bottom of the batter. Spoon into greased muffin tins, or paper cups. Sprinkle with a little sugar (it makes a frosted glaze). Bake at 375° F (190° C) for about 25 minutes or until golden brown.

Freezing Blueberries

Blueberries freeze well without sugar but retain better flavor if lightly coated with sugar: about 1/2 cup (125 mL) for every qt (L) of fruit. Freeze in freezer containers. These are excellent in blueberry muffins.

Cape Breton blueberry muffins

Chokecherries

Chokecherries grow from coast to coast in North America along the banks of streams. Its dark purple fruit is small and grows in grapelike clusters. The berries, which ripen in early fall, are inedible raw, but they make fine jellies and sasses. *Prunus, or virginiana* Midnight Schubert, with deep wine-red leaves, is an attractive non-suckering variety worth looking for.

This recipe originated when Jigs was the Jelly King. We knew nothing about whether fruits were high or low in pectin. Jigs found this recipe, it used apples, and it worked. We wouldn't have had a spare penny to buy commercial pectin, in any case.

Chokecherry-Apple Jelly

Makes about 2 pt (1 L)
2 qt chokecherries (2 L)
2 cups water (500 mL)
3 1/4 lb chopped apples (1.5 kg)
Sugar

In a large preserving pot, combine ripe chokecherries and tart fresh apples. Simmer, covered, until soft, stirring as necessary to prevent sticking. Strain mixture through a jelly bag [p. 28] and let drip for several hours or overnight.

Measure juice and cook 4 cups (1 L) at a time in a large stainless-steel pot. Bring to a boil, covered, and stir in 1 cup (250 mL) sugar to each cup (250 mL) juice. Bring to a rolling boil and, skimming as necessary, boil, uncovered, until a small amount sheets off a metal spoon [p. 28-29].

Remove jelly from heat and let subside. Stir, skimming if desired. Fill hot scalded jars [p. 28] to 1/4 inch (5 mm) from the top and seal at once with snap lids and screw bands. Process in a boiling-water bath [p. 26] or steam canner for 10 minutes.

Variation: To make *chokecherry-apple sass,* follow directions for chokecherry-apple jelly. After juice is brought to a boil, stir in 112 cup (125 mL) sugar to each cup (250 mL) juice. Boil, uncovered, until thick. Let subside. Jar and seal with snap lids and screw bands. Fill hot scalded jars [p. 28] to 1/4 inch (5 mm) from the top and seal at once with snap lids and screw bands. Process in a boiling-water bath [p. 26] or steam canner for 15 minutes.

Cranberries

There are two kinds of cranberries to harvest from the wild, *Vaccinium macrocarpon,* the bog cranberry, and *Viburnum trilobum,* high-bush cranberry. They are unrelated, but they share characteristics. They both bear acid fruit high in natural pectin. Bog cranberries are the kind served on Thanksgiving. We well remember picking bog cranberries on the shores

Cranberry Jelly

Makes about 2 pt (1 L)

1 qt bog or high-bush cranberries (1 L)
2 cups water (500 mL)
2 cups sugar (500 mL)

In a large stainless-steel pot, combine cranberries and water. Simmer, covered, until skins of cranberries crack or pop. Put hot fruit through a food mill. Add sugar and bring mixture to a boil. Skimming as necessary, boil, uncovered, about for 5 minutes.

Remove jelly from heat and let subside. Stir, skimming if desired. Fill hot scalded jars [p. 28] to 1/4 inch (5 mm) from the top and seal at once with snap lids and screw bands. Process in a boiling-water bath [p. 26] or steam canner for 10 minutes.

Cranberry Preserves

These are easier to make than the traditional cranberry jelly. If you prefer jam to jelly, chances are you will prefer these preserves.

Makes about 1 qt (1 L)

1 qt bog cranberries (1 L)
2 cups water (500 mL)
1 1/2 cups sugar (375 mL)

In a large stainless-steel pot, combine cranberries, sugar, and water. Cover and bring to a boil. Uncover and, stirring occasionally, cook slowly for about 10 minutes or until cranberry skins break.

Remove preserves from heat. Ladle into hot scalded jars [p. 28], leaving 1/2 inch (1 cm) headroom, and seal at once with snap lids and screw bands. Process in a boiling-water bath [p. 26] or steam canner for 15 minutes.

Cranberry Relish

This relish will keep for several months in the refrigerator. Lime gives it a piquant touch.

Makes about 1 qt (1 L)

1 qt bog cranberries (1 L)
1 lime (optional)
1 orange
1 cup sugar (250 mL)
1 lemon

Cut lime, orange, and lemon into quarters. Remove seeds but do not peel. Grind all fruit twice with a vegetable grinder or food processor, saving juice. Place in a large bowl and stir in juice and sugar thoroughly. Pack relish into tightly covered containers and chill. Freeze extra.

Note: If you include lime, make sure you use a heaping cup (250 mL) sugar.

Cranapple Juice

Apples
Sugar
Bog cranberries

Cut up desired amount of apples and place in a large preserving pot with desired amount of cranberries. Simmer, covered, until soft. Strain through a jelly bag [p. 28] and let drip for several hours or overnight.

Measure juice. Add 1 cup (250 mL) sugar to each qt (L) juice. Boil, uncovered, for 5 minutes.

Remove juice from heat. Pour into hot scalded jars [p. 28], leaving 1/2 inch (1 cm) headroom, and seal at once with snap lids and screw bands. Process in a boiling-water bath [p. 26] or steam canner for 15 minutes.

Cranapple Jelly

1 qt (1 L) juice makes about 2 pt (1 L)
Bog cranberries
Tart apples

Use equal amount of cranberries to apples. Cut up apples. In a large preserving pot, combine fruit with cold water. Simmer, covered, until soft, stirring as necessary. Strain mixture through a jelly bag [p. 28] and let drip for several hours or overnight.

Measure juice and cook 4 cups (1 L) at a time in a large stainless-steel pot. Bring juice to a boil, covered, and stir in 1 cup (250 mL) sugar to each cup (250 mL) juice. Bring to a boil again. Skimming as necessary, boil, uncovered, until a small amount sheets off a metal spoon [p.28-29]. Remove from heat and let jelly subside, skimming off froth if desired. Pour into hot scalded jars [p. 28], leaving 1/4 inch (5 mm) headroom, and seal at once with snap lids and screw bands. Process in a boiling-water bath [p. 26] or steam canner for 10 minutes.

Variation: To make *cranapple sass,* cook any proportion of apples and cranberries as above. Stir in 1/2 cup (125 mL) sugar to each cup (250 mL) juice and boil, uncovered, until mixture thickens. Pour into hot scalded jars [p. 28], leaving 1/4 inch (5 mm) headroom, and seal at once with snap lids and screw bands. Process in a boiling-water bath [p. 26] or steam canner for 10 minutes.

of Cape Breton on sunny, cold days, with the wind at our backs. Bog cranberries grow on creeping small-leaf plants that thrive in bogs and wet places, as well as in barren sandy areas. The fruit is best picked in late fall after a frost. High-bush cranberries grow mainly by walls and fences, in woods and low places. The large shrubs bear berries that are brighter in color than bog cranberries, but similar in size, and are best picked before frost. Both types grow in northern New England and eastern Canada, but high-bush cranberries are more common in the northeastern states. They are ornamental, with showy white flowers in the spring and crimson leaves in the fall, as well as clusters of gleaming bright red berries. We now grow a dwarf version to 6 ft (1.8 m).

Wild Grapes

Wild grapes grow as far north as New Brunswick, but they are more commonly found in the mid-Atlantic and southern states. If you are lucky enough to find them, pick them before someone else does— in early fall when some of the berries are still underripe. Make a jelly that you will never forget.

Original Wild Grape or Venison Jelly

THIS IS JIGS' SPECIALTY. ONCE FROSTED FRUIT IS SAID TO SPEED JELLING.

Makes 2 to 3 pt (1 to 1.5 L)

5 lb wild grapes (2.5 kg)
1/2 cinnamon stick
1 cup vinegar (250 mL)
Sugar
1 Tbsp whole cloves (15 mL)

In a large preserving pot, combine grapes, vinegar, cloves, and cinnamon stick. Stirring occasionally, simmer, covered, until grapes are soft. Mash. Strain through a jelly bag [p. 28] and let drip for several hours or overnight.

Measure juice and cook 4 cups (1 L) at a time in a large stainless-steel pot. Boil for 20 minutes, uncovered, and stir in 1 cup (250 ml) sugar to each cup (250 mL) juice. Skimming as necessary, boil rapidly until a small amount sheets off a metal spoon [p. 28-29].

Remove jelly from heat and let subside. Stir, skimming if desired. Fill hot scalded jars [p. 28] to 1/4 inch (5 mm) from the top and seal at once with snap lids and screw bands, Process in a boiling-water bath [p. 26] or steam canner for 10 minutes.

Wild Grape or Venison Jelly II

THE ORIGINAL RECIPE DID NOT CALL FOR APPLES BUT THEY HELP JELLING.

Makes about 4 1/2 pt (2.25 L)

4 qt wild grapes with stems (4 L)
6 lb tart fresh apples (3 kg)
1/4 cup whole cloves (50 mL)
1 qt cider vinegar (1 L)
1 qt water (1 L)
Sugar
1 /4 cup stick cinnamon (50 mL)

Cut up apples. In a large preserving pot, combine grapes, apples, cider vinegar, and water and spices. Simmer, covered, until fruit is soft, stirring as needed. Mash fruit. Strain mixture through a jelly bag [p. 28] and let drip for several hours or overnight

Measure juice and cook 4 cups (1 L) at a time in a large stainless-steel pot. Cover, bring to a boil. Stir in 1 cup (250 mL) sugar to each cup (250 mL) juice. Boil, uncovered, for 15 minutes or until a small amount sheets off a metal spoon [p.28-29]. Remove spice bag.

Remove jelly from heat and let subside. Stir, skimming if desired. Fill hot scalded jars [p. 28] to 1/4 inch (5 mm) from the top and seal at once with snap lids and screw bands, Process in a boiling-water bath [p. 26] or steam canner for 10 minutes.

Sumac

Several varieties of staghorn sumac, *Rhus typhina,* grow across the United States and Canada. They can be easily distinguished from poison sumac by their fuzzy red fruit—the poisonous variety carries white fruit. The red fruit is extremely acid and therefore is useful as a lemon substitute. Pick the fruiting branches in the early fall, about the same time as chokecherries and elderberries and before the expected rains damage the fruit. Even though it's considered a weed tree, staghorn sumac is a nice addition to the back of a large flower border if you have the space and the leaves turn a brilliant scarlet in fall. Dig up young shoots and plant them where they will have room to spread their attractive limbs. Some people call staghorn sumac "the velvet tree," because it has long velvety hairs on its branches.

Sumac Juice

SUBSTITUTE UNSWEETENED SUMAC JUICE FOR THE WATER IN ANY ELDERBERRY JAM, JELLY, JUICE, OR SASS RECIPE. FRUITING SUMAC STALKS WILL KEEP OVER WINTER IN A COOL, DRY PLACE, AWAY FROM DIRECT LIGHT.

Sumac
Sugar

Place desired amount of sumac heads in a large pot. Cover with water and pound and stir for about 10 minutes, until an extraction of juice is apparent. It has a nice pink color.

Strain through a jelly bag [p. 28] made of several layers of cheesecloth. Add sugar to taste, stirring well.

Appendix

Local Cooperative Extension Offices

http://www.csrees.usda.gov/Extension/

All you have to do is click on the map to find your local office. There you should be able to find answers to questions about growing fruit in your area and the best varieties (more correctly, cultivars) to meet your particular needs.

In Canada, contact your Provincial Department of Agriculture.

The Nearest U-Pick

Http://www.pickyourown.org/

This site can help you find "pick-your-own farms" in every state and in Canada. It is a wealth of information, including where to find canning equipment and ice cream machines.

HARD-TO-FIND & DWARF & SEMI-DWARF FRUIT STOCK

These plant nurseries sell, among other fruits, black and red currant, gooseberry, elderberry, and fruiting quince:

Miller Nurseries

http://millernurseries.com/

Ph: 1-800-836-9630

Miller's in New York State also offers Pink Champagne Currant (a cross between red and white currants); a good selection of semi-dwarf and dwarf fruit trees; Heirloom Apples, including Wolf River, the large ones we used to make into apple rings; Dwarf Blueberries to grow in tubs; Reliance Peach; High-bush Cranberry; and Jostaberry.

Raintree Nursery

http://www.raintreenursery.com/

Ph: 1-800-391-8892

Raintree in Washington State offers "The finest Old & New Cultivars From Around the World," including an unusually wide selection of Black Currants; ornamental Elderberries; Huckleberries; many kinds of Blueberries (including wild), and those best for the South and Pacific Northwest.

One Green World
http://onegreenworld.com/
Ph: 1-877-353-4028

One Green World in Oregon, although specializing in fruits for the Pacific Northwest climate, also offers hardy fruits, including Day Neutral Strawberries; and Honeyberry (hardy to -44 ° F), something to try if you have difficulty growing Blueberries.

Gurney's Seed & Nursery Co.
http://gurneys.com/
Ph: 513-354-1491

Gurney's in Indiana is a source for traditional fruits as well as Elderberry, Red Currant, Jostaberry, and Gooseberry, also a range of Blueberries, including a dwarf type; Strawberries and a Pyramidal Strawberry Bed to grow them in a small space; traditional and semi-dwarf and dwarf fruit trees including Apples, Peaches, and Pears.

Saskatoon Farm
http://www.saskatoonfarm.com/
Ph: 1-800-463-2113

This farm in Alberta, Canada, offers Gooseberry and Black Currant plants, as well as High-bush Cranberry, Honeyberry, the desirable Midnight Schubert Chokecherry, and even sells Chokecherry Syrup. There is a U-Pick operation on the farm.

Northern Alberta Permaculture Institute
http://napi.ca/

Here you will find an extensive listing of seed and plant sources in Canada.

Organic Insect Spray

Gardens Alive!
http://www.gardensalive.com/
Ph: 513-354-1482

Source for the fast-acting Pyola insect spray for dealing with the currant sawfly. It is available from Gurney's, too.

Hard-To-Find seeds of Citron Melon (Citrullus lanatus var. citroides):

Comstock Garden Seeds
http://comstockferre.com/
Ph: 860-571-6570

Seed Savers Exchange
http://www.seedsavers.org/
Ph: 563-382-5990

Ozark Seed Bank
http://onegarden.org/

Seeds of Diversity (Canada)
http://www.seeds.ca/

Canning Equipment & Related Items

Canning is more popular than ever before with more people putting up their own food. Check local sources first.

Lehman's

http://www.lehmans.com/

Ph: 1-888-438-5346

Located in Ohio in the heart of Amish country, this is a one-stop shop for the traditional water bath canner, canning jars (including the elegant European type), lids and rings, a hand-crank ice cream maker, hand food mill, and the hard-to-find steam canner and steam juicer.

Ace Hardware

http://www.acehardware.com/home/index.jsp

At this site you can find the Ace Hardware store nearest you. There you should be able to find canning equipment as well as jelly jars and all types of pectin.

Harvest Essentials

http://www.harvestessentials.com/capi.html

Offers a range of canning and preserving essentials as well as steam canners and a nifty hand food mill, La Petite Sauce Maker and Food Strainer.

Bernadin Home Canning (Canada)

http://www.bernardin.ca/

Ph: 905-731-3384

Everything you need for canning: water bath canner, jars, lids and rings, pectins.

Cheesemaking Supplies

New England Cheesemaking Supply Company

http://www.cheesemaking.com/

Ph: 413-397-2012

You will find what you need to make all the dairy recipes in this book, including the non-electric Yogotherm for making yogurt.

In Canada, contact **Glengarry Cheesemaking Dairy Supply** for similar items.

http://glengarrycheesemaking.on.ca/

Ph: 1-888-816-0903 or 613-347-1141

Manual Food Processor

Starfrit

http://www.starfrit.com/

I bought my Starfrit manual food processor in Canada at a local hardware store. You can get the same thing in the U.S. from http://www.amazon.com/

Small Electric Ice Cream Machines

Amazon also carries the Oster Ice Cream/Frozen Yogurt Maker, and other brands, for making small batches of sorbets and the like.

Bibliography

Ahern, Nell Giles, ed. *The Boston Globe's Chocolate Cook Book.* Boston: The Globe Newspaper Co., 1955.

Aish Ha Torah Women's Organization. *The Taste of Shabbos.* Spring Valley, N.Y.: Philipp Feldheim, 1987.

Ball Blue Book. rev. ed. Muncie: Ball Corp., 1974; 1982..

Ball Blue Book. Altrista Consumer Products. Daleville, Indiana: Jarden Home Brands, 2011.

Beeton, Isabella. *Mrs Beeton's All About Cookery.* London: Pan Books, 1963.

Bernadin Home Canning Guide. Toronto: Bernadin of Canada, 1975; 1995.

Blasberg, C. H. *Growing Strawberries in Vermont.* Vermont Agricultural Experiment Station. Pamphlet 15. Burlington, 1948.

Bowles, Ella Shannon, and Dorothy S. Towle. *Secrets of New England Cooking.* New York: M. Barrows, 1947.

Brattleboro, Vermont, Woman's Club. *My Ladye's Coke Book.* Brattleboro, 1924.

Brown, Marion. *Pickles & Preserves.* New York: Wilfred Funk, 1955.

Canada. Department of Agriculture. *Elderberry Cultivation in Eastern Canada.* Publication 1280. Ottawa, 1966.

Department of Agriculture. *Growing Red Raspberries in Eastern Canada.* Publication 1196. Ottawa, 1964.

Department of Agriculture. *Growing Strawberries in Eastern Canada.* Publication 1170. Ottawa.

Department of Agriculture. *Planting and Growing Rhubarb.* Publication 1369. Ottawa, 1968.

Claiborne, Craig. *An Herb & Spice Book.* New York: Bantam, 1963.

Downes, Muriel, and Rosemary Hume. *Jams, Preserves & Pickles.* New York: Weathervane Books.

Farmer, Fannie. *The Boston Cooking School Cook Book.* Boston, 1896.

Fernald, M. L., et al. *Edible Wild Plants of Eastern North America.* New-York: Harper & Bros., 1958.

Fraser, S. *American Fruits.* Orange Judd Co., 1924.

Fuller, A. S., *The Small Fruit Culturist.* 1867.

Gibbons, E, *Stalking the Wild Asparagus.* New York: David McKay, 1962.

Grigson, Jane, *Jane Grigson's Fruit Book.* New York: Atheneum, 1982.

"Handbook on Pruning." *Brooklyn Botanical Garden Record, Plants and Gardens,* 37, 2 (1981).

Hedrick, U. P. *Fruits for the Home Garden,* repr. New York: Dover, 1973.

Hill, Lewis. *Fruits and Berries for the Home Garden.* Garden Way, Vt., 1980.

The Home Institute of the New York Herald Tribune. *America's Cookbook.* New York: Charles Scribner's Sons, 1943.

Mosser, Marjorie. *Foods of Old New England.* Garden City: Doubleday, 1957.

The New Settlement Cookbook. New York: Simon & Schuster, 1954.

Petrides, G. A. *A Field Guide to Trees and Shrubs.* Cambridge, Mass.: Houghton Mifflin, 1958.

Ricketson, C. L. *Currants and Gooseberries.* Vineland Station, Ont.: Horticultural Research Institute of Ontario, 1966.

Sanford, S. N. F. *New England Herbs.* Boston: New England Museum of Natural History, 1937.

Shoemaker, J. S., *Small Fruit Culture.* New York: McGraw-Hill, 1955.

Vegetable Growing. New York: Wiley & Sons, 1953.

Showalter, Mary Emma. *Mennonite Community Cookbook.* Scottdale, Pa.: Herald Press, 1974.

Tompkins, J. P., and D. K. Ourecky. *Raspberry Growing in New York State.* Cornell University Extension Publication Information. Bulletin 155. Ithaca.

Tatum, Billy Joe. *Wild Foods Field Guide and Cookbook.* New York: Workman, 1976.

Two-Hundred Favorite Recipes of The Cape Breton Bicentennial Dancers. Winnipeg, Manitoba: Gateway Publishing Co. Ltd.

United States. Department of Agriculture. *Strawberry Varieties in the U.S.* Farmers' Bulletin 1043. Washington, D.C., 1958.

Wyman, D. *Wyman's Gardening Encyclopedia.* New York: Macmillan, 1972.

Index

Notes